HOLIDAY PLASTIC NOVELTIES
THE STYRENE TOYS

CHARLENE PINKERTON
PHOTOGRAPHY BY RON PINKERTON

4880 Lower Valley Road, Atglen, PA 19310 USA

Dedicated to
Jordan Christopher Shock

ACKNOWLEDGMENTS

There are many people who help on a project like this. Friends opened up their homes for us to take pictures in. Others offered photographs and help at the flea markets. Still others purchased toys at their own expense to be used in pictures for this book. Bertram M. Cohen packaged up his collection and sent it through the mail to be photographed when our trip to Boston was canceled. Mark Craven and Richard Miller took many of their own pictures, which was very helpful. I thank my husband and son for helping me with everything and putting up with all the extra work. Many more thanks and appreciation to the following people:

Kathleen and Christian Eric, Don Featherstone, Union Products, Bertram M. Cohen, Irwin Plastic Corporation, Keith Lauer, Marshall Naul, Tracy Whitney, Richard Miller, Mark and Judy Craven, Joan Manning, Bryon Foot, Ginny and Dave Wellington, Phil Dimaggio, Ken Stebenne, Morris Novelties, Carol Thompson, Cynthia Watson, Suzy and Dale Thomas, Bill Meyers, Peter Schiffer, Joel Berman, Randy Pinkerton, Fran Pinkerton, Tom Weber, Beverly Archer, Bill Altfather, Bob Lansion, Tana DeRenzo, Lee Wellington, Joy Pinegan, Steve Effnor at P.C.C., Bea DeArmond, Ann Davidson, Larry Tyler, Ken Kealey, and Elizabeth Fitzgerald.

Book Design by Anne Davidsen
Type set in Zapf Humanst 601 BT /Aldine 701 BT

ISBN: 0-7643-0781-9
Printed in China

Published by Schiffer Publishing Ltd.
4880 Lower Valley Road
Atglen, PA 19310
Phone: (610) 593-1777; Fax: (610) 593-2002
E-mail: Schifferbk@aol.com
Please visit our web site catalog at **www.schifferbooks.com**

This book may be purchased from the publisher.
Include $3.95 for shipping.
Please try your bookstore first.
We are interested in hearing from authors
with book ideas on related subjects.
You may write for a free catalog.

In Europe, Schiffer books are distributed by
Bushwood Books
6 Marksbury Rd.
Kew Gardens
Surrey TW9 4JF England
Phone: 44 (0)181 392-8585; Fax: 44 (0)181 392-9876
E-mail: Bushwd@aol.com

CONTENTS

FOREWORD

The mass produced holiday novelty toy became very popular in America during the last half of the nineteenth century. At that time, our novelties came mostly from Germany or Europe. They were made of papier-mâché, bisque, wood, or metal. In the early twentieth century, more novelties were beginning to be made in the United States as well as in Germany and Japan, and were beginning to be made out of such plastics as bakelite, celluloid, polystyrene, and many other plastics. In the late 1930s and 1940s, plastic injection molding of styrene became popular for novelties made for the holidays. During WW II, these styrene toys continued to be made on a small scale. After WW II, styrene was used for all kinds of holiday novelty toys, including candy containers, holiday lights and decoration, banks, party favors, baby toys, and stocking stuffers, as well as inexpensive picnic and party ware and novelty kitchen decorations. This book is about the novelties that flourished at the end of the art deco era. Those wonderful, good quality hard plastic novelty items were sold in dime stores, drug stores, department stores, and candy counters across the United States. They filled our holidays and other festive occasions with extra joy as we counted them among our treasures.

INTRODUCTION

Many years ago at the Rose Bowl Fleamarket in Southern California, I was looking through a box for treasures at the end of the day. At the bottom, I came across a baby toy that I once had as a small child. It was a plastic Knickerbocker whale bath tub toy. The feeling of nostalgia that came across me was overwhelming. I gave the man a quarter and went on my way. I had not considered plastic collecting at that time; collectors were not into plastic. At first I thought about buying it only for resale, but I was extremely attracted to the bright colors, and the more I bought the more I kept for myself. I soon noticed that the inexpensive plastic toys of my childhood were extremely well made, and the designs were beautifully matched to the late art deco period in which I grew up.

The late 1940s and 1950s were a great time to grow up in. The United States had just finished with WW II, and our parents came home from the war. A time of prosperity was at hand. During this time, the plastics industry was beginning to develop many more uses for plastic than ever before. We became a disposable nation. We lived with the idea that plastic was cheap, so if it breaks we'll throw it away and get a new one. Eventually, we created environmental problems for the world. Today we have plastics that can be recycled into new items, instead of being thrown away. We have learned how to care for the environment. Collectors are helping to do their share by collecting plastics and saving them for the next generations to enjoy.

READERS PLEASE NOTICE: The prices in this book have been compiled after many years of collecting, buying, and selling old plastic toys and dolls. Those prices do not always reflect the sometimes inflated eBay auction prices on the Internet.

Also, the "Toys" section has been divided into four categories: Christmas; Easter; Valentine's, Halloween, and Thanksgiving; and Other Occasions. Sometimes, in order to show how the same novelty was used for different occasions, an example will be shown out of category.

New reproduction Rosen cart and wheels (notice new axle and different mold mark than rear of original platform). Showing inverted "V" mold mark, old axle and wheels, Knickerbocker Rooster on new Rosen platform. Showing old Tico Toys snowman on new Rosen platform.

THE STYRENE NOVELTY TOYS

THE HARD PLASTIC TOYS
MADE IN THE U.S.A.: THE 1940S TO 1950S

The polystyrene injection molded toys produced by the plastic toy companies during the 1940s and the 1950s gave us a toy that was much more durable than celluloid. There were hundreds of thousands of these toys that were produced and were used as decorations or given for presents. Styrene molding began in the late 1930s and escalated after WW II, giving us beautifully colored hard plastic novelties that would outlast many other kinds of toys produced. The only problem with the styrenes is that they had a tendency to shatter into pointed harmful pieces when broken. Consumer safety demanded a more durable plastic than styrene. Irwin Cohn, of the Irwin Plastic Corporation, was one of the first people to produce polyethylene or vinyl injection molded toys that equaled their steel counter parts in play, value, and strength. In the 1940s, Mr. Cohn and his employees threw the polyethylene toys around their show room in New York City to demonstrate the plastic's strength.

Although polyethylene was used during the 1940s for some toys, polystyrene was the most popular of the plastics. The new polyethylene vinyl had a tendency to decompose, and it would be many years before a good hard vinyl toy would hit the toy markets. There were many other types of plastic that were used during the 1940s and

1950s. However the styrenes prevailed as the plastic symbol of that time. It was a time when most American toys were made in the U.S.A. Today is a very modern and sophisticated time of design, marketing, and production in the plastic toy industry, compared to the less complicated post-World War II era, before toys were advertised on TV and marketed for movies.

REPRODUCTIONS OF OLD STYRENE

There have been reproductions of E. Rosen candy containers, carts, and wheels showing up on the collectors' market and sold over the internet. This is a good reason for new collectors of plastic to be wary of what they buy. Get to know company designs, old plastic wear marks, company embossments, and where they are located on the toys. Axles that are made of metal can be made to look old by rusting outdoors. For the most part, old styrene remains shiny, but becomes somewhat brittle and fragile with age. In contrast, reproduction toys usually have a dull finish because the correct type of plastic was not used. Remember, it is possible to copy a mold and create an old looking plastic toy, but this procedure would be time consuming and will cause the resultant toy to be expensive. The price of the item would start high on the collectible market, instead of growing in value at a steady pace as a good original collectible should do.

THE MAIN MANUFACTURERS OF PLASTIC HOLIDAY TOYS

THE KNICKERBOCKER PLASTIC COMPANY INC.

The Knickerbocker Plastic Company, Inc., made extremely good quality hard plastic Easter and all occasion novelty toys and dolls. Their pieces are thick and shiny. The Easter designs have a charming country look to them. The animals are dressed in clothes and ready for farm work. They made their toys in graduated sizes and different combinations of primary colors. They made pigs, ducks, roosters, chickens, and bunnies. The company began in Glendale, California. The address was at 4101 San Fernando Drive in Glendale. There was a show room at 1107 Broadway in New York. This company was not related to the famous L.L. Knickerbocker Toy Company. The L.L. Knickerbocker Toy Company believes that many business used their name because it was such a prestigious name coming out of the late nineteenth century. Knickerbocker Plastic Company Toys have different embossments on them. Some of the early toys are not embossed. Some are em-

bossed North Hollywood and others Glendale, California.

The Knickerbocker Plastic Company disappears after the 1950s. It could have been bought out by another company. There are no toys made after the 1950s of newer plastic material with their name on them. There were Knickerbocker Plastic Company novelty dolls reproduced unmarked or made in Hong Kong during the 1960s. These dolls were used for many years by Native American Indians and Eskimos, dressed in their native costumes, and sold for souvenirs.

The artists that designed the Knickerbocker toys could have been involved with the company in other ways. They could have been employees who had exceptional drawing talent and were asked to submit designs. They could have been company owners. This type of artistic procedure takes place even today in novelty companies. Good artistic records have not always been kept in the American Novelty Toy business.

The E. Rosen Candy Company

The Ephrain Rosen Candy Company began business in 1911. They are truly an American institution when it comes to the American sweet tooth. Those great child pacifiers—novelty toys and surprises—have given children great joy throughout the years. Still in business today, E. Rosen Company is headed by Harris Rosen in Providence, Rhode Island. Rosbro Plastics was a factory separate from the candy company, where novelty toys were made out of styrene during the 1940s and 1950s. Both companies are owned by the Rosen family. E. Rosen bought out the Tico Toys Novelty Company in 1946. The Tico Toys Novelty Company made unmarked inexpensive novelties during the 1940s. These toys were ordered and sold by other businesses, who wanted to increase their holiday novelty sales. Sears, The Miller Electric Company, and the Royal Light Company as well as many other businesses bought novelties made in the Pawtucket, Providence, Rhode Island area. The unmarked toys you find can be either Tico Toys or early Rosen. They used many of the same molds.

The E. Rosen candy containers have an Art Deco look to them. Bugs Bunny®, that lovable cartoon rabbit with the long ears and smart aleck attitude; those witches on the old motorcycles; the early rockets; jets; and the early television camera all came out of the late 1940s. The smoking characters are characteristic of the 1940s, as well. Frosty the Snowman® and Rudolph the Red Nose Reindeer® are characters that come out of the late 1930s and 1940s.

The Irwin Corporation

Irwin Cohn is considered to be one of the great plastic toy innovators of his time. The Irwin Corporation began in 1922 and ended in 1973. Mr. Cohn died in 1970. Mr. Cohn and L. Marx were the same age and both were involved in the plastics industry. In 1973 Bertram Cohen, the son-in-law of Irwin Cohn, sold the company. He had gone to work for his father-in-law in 1957. Bert is now retired and is a collector of marbles and other memorabilia. He organizes marble tournaments all over the world.

Irwin Cohn used all of the modern methods he pioneered himself to make styrene blow-molded toys. This was a type of production where the polystyrene was blown into the molds.

During WW II, Irwin Cohn used sources that were not critically necessary for the war effort. He used molding powder made of scrap cloth to produce plastic novelty toys. Eventually the Irwin Corporation became one of the most successful toy companies in the world. At one time, they employed 800 people and were engaged in all facets of production. They made plastic raw materials and manufactured finished toys. This was a great accomplishment for a company that began by making celluloid boxes to hold soap in a small room in Leominster, Massachusetts, a city that became the plastics capital of the United States.

The company moved from Leominster to Fitchburg, Massachusetts, and then eventually to Nashua, New Hampshire. The sales arm of the business was in New York City at 200 Fifth Ave. There were two large plastic toy molding factories, one was at 85 Factory St., Nashua, New Hampshire. The other large factory was in Leominster. The Irwin toys were made by Great American Plastics Company, an affiliate of the Irwin Corporation at these two locations. Another company affiliate was the Great American Chemical Corporation that produced the raw materials. Mr. Cohn was president and chairman of all the companies. His wife, Mary, was the corporation treasurer and helped with the toy designs. Mr. Cohn was very active in his community. He loved animals and bred dogs that he entered in dog shows around the country. He gave money to many charities, and was involved in social and religious activities in Leominster, Massachusetts.

Union Products

Union Products manufactured plastic Halloween novelties from the early 1950s into the 1960s. They made good quality toys, among them the popular witch #305 and the battery and electrically operated lanterns and lights. Union Products used styrene for their novelties into the early 1960s. Now they use good quality hard vinyl.

In the 1960s they discontinued their Halloween line, but during the 1980s, they began to manufacture all holiday items. This company also makes all types of lawn decorations, lawn furniture, flower pots, and saucers. They also make the famous pink flamingo lawn decoration.

The company is located in Leominster, Massachusetts. It is an American owned business. Don Featherstone is a collector and also a co-owner of the company. He designs some of the holiday lawn ornaments and lights. They are embossed with his name and a date. Don is the first person to personalize holiday plastic. Union products is one of the leading manufactures of holiday lights and lawn decorations in the United States.

E. Rosen/Tico Toys, Santa coming out of chimney candy container, late 1940s, older looking Santa, not embossed. Red plastic, face painted flesh color, white and black paint, 5" x 3". *Author's Collection.* $75-95.

E. Rosen Santa on motorcycle candy container, late 1940s, not embossed. Green and red plastic, white and black paint, 3.25" x 3.75". *Author's Collection.* $85-100.

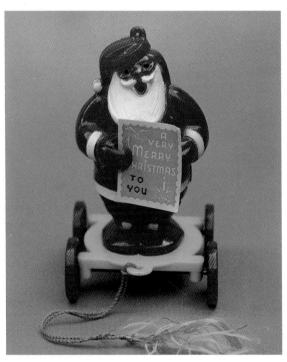

E. Rosen Santa on a platform candy container, 1950s, not embossed. This Santa was used for many years; the greeting card says "Merry Christmas and Happy New Year, The E. Rosen Candy Company." Red and green plastic, white and black paint, 4.5" x 2.25". *Author's Collection.* $45-65.

E. Rosen Santa on a platform holding a tree, candy container, 1950s, not embossed. Red and green plastic, white, flesh and black paint, 4.5" x 2.25". *Author's Collection.* $45-65.

Boxed E. Rosen plastic toys with pops. *Courtesy of Mark and Judy Craven. Photo by Mark Craven.* $275-325.

Santa's five star candy special box, showing different Rosen characters. $275-325.

E. Rosen Santa with sleigh candy container, 1950s, not embossed. Red and green plastic, white and black paint, 3.25" x 4.5". *Courtesy of Richard Miller. Photo by Richard Miller.* $45-65.

mint 15 ✓

Tico Toys hanging Santa ornament, late 1940s, not embossed (note the beard is slightly different than the E. Rosen Santa's). Red plastic, white paint, 3.5" x 2". *Author's Collection.* $35-50.

E. Rosen Santa holding a broom on a platform candy container, 1950s, not embossed. Red and green plastic, white and black paint, 4.5" x 2.25". *Courtesy of Suzy and Dale Thomas.* $45-65.

E. Rosen Tool Santa hanging ornament, early 1950s, not embossed. Red and green plastic, white, flesh and blue paint, 4" x 2.5". *Author's Collection.* $55-75.

E. Rosen Tool Santa hanging ornaments, early 1950s, not embossed. Basic Santas are blue, red, and purple plastic with white, flesh, red, and blue paint, 4" x 2.5". *Courtesy of Suzy and Dale Thomas.* $55-75 each.

E. Rosen Tool Santa on platform with ax candy container, 1950s, not embossed. Red, green, and yellow plastic with white and black paint, 4.5" x 2.25". *Courtesy of Suzy and Dale Thomas.* $55-75.

E. Rosen Tool Santa hanging ornaments, early 1950s, not embossed. Basic Santas are yellow, blue, and green plastic with white, flesh, red, and blue paint, 4" x 2.5". *Courtesy of Suzy and Dale Thomas. $55-75 each*.

E. Rosen Santa and reindeer sleigh candy container, 1950s, not embossed, boxed for Sears and Roebuck and Company Chicago, Ill., and other leading cities. Box is 15" x 5". *Author's Collection. $65-85.*

E. Rosen Santa with two reindeer sleigh candy container, 1950s, not embossed. Red, white, and green plastic with white and black paint.16" x 5". *Courtesy of Suzy and Dale Thomas. $45-65.*

E. Rosen Santa's Candy Wagon, 1950s, not embossed. White, red, yellow, and green plastic with white, flesh, red and black paint. 9.5" x 8". *Courtesy of Cynthia Watson. $150-175.*

E. Rosen Santa holding wreath candy container, 1950s, not embossed. Red, white, and black plastic with white, flesh, green, and red paint. 10.75" x 7". *Courtesy of Richard Miller. Photo by Richard Miller. $85-100.*

E. Rosen Santa with horn candy container, 1950s, not embossed. Red and yellow plastic, with white, flesh, and black paint. He is standing on heavy cardboard base that shows ingredients and shows the E. Rosen Candy Company name. 5.5" x 3.5". *Author's Collection. $55-70.*

E. Rosen Santa Elf standing inside of a wreath candy container, 1950s, not embossed. Red and green plastic, with white, flesh, black, and red paint, 8.5" x 8". *Courtesy of Richard Miller. Photo by Richard Miller. $45-65.*

E. Rosen Santa Elf candy containers, 1950s, not embossed. Red plastic with white, flesh, and black paint. Bending over Elf is 3.75" x 3". Elf with suspenders is 4.25" x 3". *Author's Collection. $30-45 each.*

E. Rosen Santa Elf standing on platform holding a stocking, candy container, 1950s, not embossed. Red and green plastic with white, flesh, and black paint. 4.75" x 3.5". *Courtesy of Suzy and Dale Thomas. $45-65.*

E. Rosen Santa Elf on platform holding a stocking, candy container, 1950s, not embossed. Red and green plastic with white, flesh, and black paint. 4.5" x 3.5". *Courtesy of Suzy and Dale Thomas. $45-65.*

E. Rosen Santa with horn and elves sleigh with an Irwin Reindeer candy, container, 1950s, not embossed. White, green, and red plastic with black, white, and flesh paint. 12" x 3". *Courtesy of Mark and Judy Craven. $125-250.*

E. Rosen Christmas cat candy container, 1950s, not embossed, rare. Red plastic with white paint, very rare color, 5" x 3.5". *Courtesy of Richard Miller. Photo by Richard Miller. $55-65.*

E. Rosen Santa Elf riding a reindeer candy container, 1950s, not embossed. Red and white plastic with white, flesh, and black paint, 6" x 3.5". *Courtesy of Suzy and Dale Thomas. $45-65.*

E. Rosen Christmas candy/ surprise ornaments, 1960s, tagged E. Rosen Candy Company. Red, green and blue plastic with clear plastic tops. 2" in diameter. *Author's Collection. $10 each.*

Smoking snowman carrying a lantern light, 1940s, not embossed. White and black plastic with red and black paint. 6.75" x 4". *Author's Collection and author's favorite.* $65-85.

E. Rosen Jolly Skater candy container, 1950s, embossed Rosbro Plastics. White, blue, and green plastic, with red, blue, and flesh paint. 5" x 3" *Author's Collection. $65-85.*

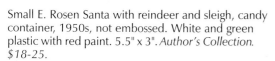

Small E. Rosen Santa with reindeer and sleigh, candy container, 1950s, not embossed. White and green plastic with red paint. 5.5" x 3". *Author's Collection. $18-25.*

E. Rosen Christmas and Halloween snowmen, 1950s , embossed Rosbro Plastics. White and orange plastic with red, black, and white paint. 5" x 3". *Author's Collection. White snowman is $25- 40, Halloween snowman is $150.*

E. Rosen Snowman with glasses and umbrella, candy container, 1950s, embossed Rosbro Plastics. White and black plastic with red paint. 5" x 3". *Author's Collection. $45-65.*

NO GLASSES

Jolly Skater light with original box, 1950s, embossed Rosbro Plastics. White, yellow, silver, and blue plastic, with red, blue, and flesh paint. 5" x 3". *Courtesy of Richard Miller. Photo by Richard Miller. $100-125.*

E. Rosen Snowman with broom and shovel, candy container, 1950s, embossed Rosbro Plastics. White, black, red, and yellow plastic with black and red paint. 5" x 3.25". *Author's Collection. $45-65.*

E. Rosen/Tico Toys Snowman candy container and Halloween pirate candy container, late 1940s-1950s, not embossed. White and orange plastic with green, black, red paint. 3" x 2.50". *Author's Collection.* The Halloween pirate is worth $65, the Snowman $15-25.

Snowman not embossed, 1950s. Made in U.S.A. White plastic with red and black paint. 4" x 2". *Author's Collection.* $15-20.

E. Rosen/Tico Toy Snowman candy container and Halloween cat candy container, late 1940s-1950s not embossed. White, orange, and black plastic with yellow, red, black, and white paint. 3" x 2.50". *Courtesy of Richard Miller. Photo by Richard Miller.* Cat is $65, snowman $10-15.

Frosty the Snowman record center disc, 1940s. The Snowman goes around while the record is playing. The disc says Copyright Hill and Range Songs Incorporated, New York. The Snowman measures 3" x 1.50", came from Pawtucket, Providence, Rhode Island area. *Author's Collection.* $65-85.

E. Rosen Snowman candy container on wheels, not embossed. . Made in U.S.A. White, black, and green plastic with blue, black, and red paint. *Courtesy of Mark and Judy Craven. Photo by Mark Craven. $85-100 rare.*

Snowman Light, 1950s, not embossed. Made in U.S.A. White and black plastic with green, red, and black paint, 11" x 4". *Courtesy of Richard Miller. $45-65.*

Miller Electric Company Snowman Light, 1940s and 1950s, embossed Rosbro plastics from the Pawtucket, Rhode Island area. White and black plastic with red and black paint. *Courtesy of Carol Thompson. $55-75.*

Front of box for the Snowman Light.

Irwin Snowman with top hat, late 1940s, embossed Irwin Plastics. White plastic with red paint. 3.50" x 1.34". *Courtesy of Suzy and Dale Thomas. $20-35.*

Irwin Snowman with stocking cap, late 1940s, embossed Irwin Plastics. White plastic with red and black paint. 3.50" x 1.34". *Courtesy of Suzy and Dale Thomas. $20-35.*

Early plastic Santa with long coat, 1940s. Made in U.S.A. He is a bank and a hanging ornament. He is not embossed and at one time carried something in his hand. He is red plastic with white paint. 6" x 3". *Author's Collection. $65-85.*

Early plastic Santa with long coat, 1940s. Made in U.S.A. He is also a bank and a hanging ornament. Clear plastic with red and white paint. 6" x 3". *Author's Collection. $65-85.*

1950s Santa on reindeer made with rabbit's fur, not embossed. Made in U.S.A. He is white plastic with red, flesh color, with black and rose paint. 6" x 7.50". *Courtesy of Suzy and Dale Thomas.* $35-45.

1950s Santa made with rabbit's fur. He is a hanging ornament and the toys at his feet were carried in a bag over his shoulder, not embossed. Made in U.S.A. White plastic with red, flesh color, white, and black paint. 6" x 3.50". *Courtesy of Suzy and Dale Thomas.* $40-55.

E. Rosen HiHo Santa figure light, electrified by the Miller Electric Company. This Santa is not embossed. White plastic with red, flesh, white, and black paint. 10" x 11". *Author's Collection.* $85-120.

E. Rosen Santa riding reindeer on wheels candy container. White plastic with red, green, yellow, tan, and flesh paint. 10" by 11". *Courtesy of Mark and Judy Craven. Photo by Mark Craven. $85-120*

E. Rosen Santa riding reindeer on wheels candy container. White, green, and yellow plastic with red, black, white, and flesh paint. 10" by 11". *Courtesy of Mark and Judy Craven. Photo by Mark Craven. $15-25.*

E. Rosen Santa sucker holder, 1950s, not embossed. White plastic with red paint. 5" x 2.50". *Author's Collection. $15-25.*

Jack and Jill chow feeding train with Tico Toys elves, 1940s and 1950s. The elves are not embossed. The train was made by B. W. Molded Plastics, Pasadena, California. The train plastic is called flex ware, the fork and spoon inside of the cup are molded. *Author's Collection. Train $85-100, the elves are $15-25 each.*

21

Tico Toys tugboat Christmas candy whistle, candy container, 1940s, not embossed. Red and green plastic. 4.50" x 2.50", rare. *Author's Collection. $65-85.*

Irwin elf hanging ornament, late 1940s, embossed Irwin Plastics. Red plastic with yellow paint. 3" x 2". *Courtesy of Bertram M. Cohen, Irwin Plastics Corporation.*

E. Rosen Santa in yellow sled candy container, 1950s, not embossed. Yellow and red plastic with white and black paint, 5" x 3". *Courtesy of Suzy and Dale Thomas. $25-40.*

Santa in a jet racecar 1950s . Made in U.S.A. Red and white plastic. 2.75" by 1.75". *Courtesy of Mark and Judy Craven, Photo by Mark Craven. $45-65.*

E. Rosen Santa in cart, candy container, 1950s, not embossed. White, green, and yellow plastic with white and black paint, 7.50" x 5.34". *Courtesy of Suzy and Dale Thomas.* $65-95.

E. Rosen Santa in green sleigh candy container, 1950s, not embossed. Green and red plastic with white and black paint, 5" x 3". *Author's Collection.* $25-40

Santa in a car, candy container, E. Rosen, 1950s. Green, yellow, and red plastic with white and black paint, 6.50" x 3". *Courtesy of Suzy and Dale Thomas.* $95-125.

E. Rosen/Tico Toys hanging Santa ornament, candy container, late 1940s and 1950s, not embossed. This Santa matches the small Snowman and Halloween pirate and is probably a mate to a set of ornaments. Red plastic with black and white paint, 3.50" x 2". *Author's Collection.* $15-25.

E. Rosen Santa in a car, candy container, 1950s. Car is embossed Rosbro Plastics. White and red plastic with black and white paint, 7.50" x 3.50". *Author's Collection. $95-125.*

E. Rosen/Tico Toys Christmas giraffe, candy container, late 1940s-1950s, not embossed. Tan and red plastic with brown paint and original cord tail, rare, 7.50" x 5.50". *Author's Collection. $135-165.*

E. Rosen/Tico Toys Christmas giraffe, candy container, late 1940s-1950s, not embossed. Red and green plastic with white paint with original cord tail, rare, 7.50" x 5.50". *Courtesy of Suzy and Dale Thomas $135-165.*

E. Rosen/Tico Toys Easter giraffe, candy container, late 1940s-1950s, not embossed. Pink and yellow plastic with green paint and original cord tail, rare, 7.50" x 5.50". *Courtesy of Suzy and Dale Thomas. $135-165.*

E. Rosen Santas on skis candy containers, 1950s, embossed Rosbro Plastics. Red and Green Plastic with white and black paint, 4.50" x 4.50" each. *Courtesy of Carol Thompson. $30-45 each.*

E. Rosen Santa on skis carrying a stocking, candy container, 1950s, embossed Rosbro Plastics. Red, green, and white plastic with white, red, and black paint, 4.50" x 4.50". *Courtesy of Richard Miller. Photo by Richard Miller. $35-50.*

E. Rosen Santa on snowshoes candy container. He did have something in his hand, 1950s, embossed Rosbro Plastics. Red and white plastic with black and white paint, 4.50" x 3.50". *Author's Collection. $30-45.*

Santa on skis light, electrified by the Miller Electric Company, 1950s, Pawtucket, Rhode Island, embossed Rosbro Plastics. *Author's Collection. $40-65.*

Santa on skis hanging ornament candy container Irwin style, 1950s, not embossed. Made in U.S.A. Green and red plastic with white paint, 4" x 4". *Courtesy of Suzy and Dale Thomas. $20-30.*

Santa on skis hanging ornament and candy container, late 1940s, not embossed, probably Tico Toys or early Irwin. Green and red plastic with white and black paint, 5" x 4". *Author's Collection. $35-45.*

Santa on skis tree ornament, 1940s, early un-marked Irwin Plastics. Red and white plastic with white paint, 4" x 3". *Author's Collection. $20-35.*

E. Rosen/Tico Toys Christmas telephone, candy container, rare, late 1940s, not embossed. Red plastic with original cord and metal receiver holder, 4.50" x 1.50". *Author's Collection. $50-65.*

E. Rosen/Tico Toys Christmas telephone, candy container, rare, late 1940s, not embossed. Green plastic with original cord and metal receiver holder, 4.50" x 1.50". *Courtesy of Suzy and Dale Thomas. $50-65.*

E. Rosen Christmas donkey candy container, late 1940s and 1950s, not embossed. Red and black plastic with pink, yellow, green, white, and black paint. He has a silver painted muzzle, all original, 4.50" x 5.50". *Author's Collection. $135-165.*

E. Rosen Easter donkey candy container, late 1940s and 1950s, not embossed. Yellow and green plastic with green paint with original tassel, 4.50" x 5.50". *Author's Collection. $135-165*

Tico Toy Christmas car, candy container, late 1940s, not embossed. Green and red plastic, 4" x 1.75. *Author's Collection. $35-50.*

E. Rosen Halloween donkey candy container, late 1940s and 1950s, not embossed. Orange and black plastic with black paint, 4.50" x 5.50". *Courtesy of Dave and Ginny Wellington. $150-175.*

E. Rosen Trojan horse Valentine candy container, 1950s, embossed Rosbro Plastics. Pink marbled and red plastic original tassel and tag, 5" x 5.50". *Courtesy of Suzy and Dale Thomas. $65-85.*

E. Rosen Trojan horse candy container, 1950s, embossed Rosbro Plastics. Clear and green plastic with red paint, 5" x 5.50". *Courtesy of Mark and Judy Craven. $65-85.*

Two E. Rosen Trojan horse Christmas candy containers, 1950s, embossed Rosbro Plastics. Red and green plastic with black paint, 5" x 5.50". *Author's Collection. $65-85, each.*

E. Rosen Trojan horse candy containers, Christmas and Halloween, 1950s, embossed Rosbro Plastics. The Christmas horse is clear and green plastic with a painted red saddle and bridle. The Halloween horse is black and orange plastic with white paint, 5" x 5.50". *Author's Collection. Christmas horse is $65-85, Halloween horse $50-85.*

E. Rosen Trojan horse candy container for Easter, 1950s, embossed Rosbro Plastics. Yellow and green plastic with black paint, 5" x 5.50". *Author's Collection. $50-65.*

E. Rosen Trojan horse candy container for Easter, 1950s, embossed Rosbro Plastics. Cream color and yellow plastic, 5" x 5.50". *Author's Collection. $50-65.*

E. Rosen Christmas boot candy container, 1950s, embossed Rosbro Plastic. Red and green plastic, 4" x 2.50". *Author's Collection. $25-45.*

Three different sizes of E. Rosen boot candy containers. The tallest boot is embossed Rosbro Plastic. The other two are tagged E. Rosen Candy Company and embossed Rosbro Plastics. Red plastic, from L to R, 4", 3", 2". *Author's Collection. $10,5,5.*

E. Rosen/Tico Toy marching soldier candy containers, late 1940s-1950s, not embossed. Yellow and white plastic with green and red paint. The green and yellow soldier could have been made for Easter too, 4" x 1.50". *Courtesy of Richard Miller. Photo by Richard Miller. $18-25, each.*

E. Rosen/Tico Toy marching soldier candy containers, late 1940s-1950s, not embossed. White and yellow plastic with green and blue paint, 4" x 1.50". *Courtesy of Richard Miller. Photo by Richard Miller. $18-25.*

E. Rosen/Tico Toys bear bank, candy container pull toy, late 1940s, not embossed. Tan, yellow, and green plastic with red paint, 5" x 1.75". *Courtesy of Suzy and Dale Thomas. $65-85.*

E. Rosen/Tico Toys bear bank, late 1940s, not embossed. White plastic with blue paint, 4" x 1.75". *Author's Collection. $45-65.*

Irwin Santa candy container, late 1940s-1950s, embossed Irwin plastics. Red plastic with white paint, 6" x 3". *Courtesy of Bertram M. Cohen, Irwin Plastics Corporation Estate Collection. $25-45.*

Six Santa hanging ornament candy containers, late 1940s-1950s, not embossed, they are probably early Irwin unmarked toys. Red plastic with black and white paint, 4" x 2". *Author's Collection. $20-35 each.*

Single Irwin Santa and sleigh candy container, 1950s, embossed Irwin plastics. White and red plastic with white paint, 5" x 3.5". *Courtesy of Carol Thompson. $20-35.*

Identical Irwin Santa's, 1950s, embossed Irwin Plastics. Santa on left is flash red with white paint. The one on right is red plastic with white paint. *Author's Collection. $8-15.*

Irwin Santa two reindeer sleigh in box named "The Reindeer Barn," 1950s, embossed Irwin Plastics. Red and white plastic with white paint, the box is 12" x 4". *Courtesy of Suzy and Dale Thomas. $45-60.*

broken sled

Irwin Santa in two reindeer sleigh, 1950s, embossed Irwin Plastics. Red and white plastic with white paint, 10" x 4.50". *Courtesy of Carol Thompson. $25-40.*

Irwin Santa and four reindeer with sleigh on platform, late 1940s-1950s. These reindeer are of a different style. Santa and the sleigh are also of a different style, embossed Irwin Plastics. *Courtesy of Suzy and Dale Thomas $35-50.*

Irwin silver and gold flash single reindeer sleigh on a platform, 1950s, embossed Irwin Plastics. The platform is 10" x 3.50". *Courtesy of Carol Thompson. $20-30.*

Irwin silver and gold flash double reindeer sleigh on a platform, 1950s, embossed Irwin Plastics, 10" x 3.5". *Author's Collection. $25-35.*

Irwin single sleigh reindeer, late 1940s-1950s, embossed Irwin Plastics. Silver and red flash with white paint, 9" x 3". Original box with picture of children hanging stockings. *Courtesy of Suzy and Dale Thomas. $40-50.*

Donkey and elephant hanging tree ornaments, 1950s, not embossed. White plastic with red paint, donkey: 3" x 3", elephant: 3" x 2.50". *Courtesy of Suzy and Dale Thomas. $15-25 each.*

Santa light, 1950s, not embossed. Made in U.S.A. Red plastic with white, flesh, and black paint, 5" x 2". *Courtesy of Carol Thompson. $15-25.*

Two Christmas Kings, not embossed. Made in U.S.A. Painted silver, gold, red, and blue flash, 3.5" by 4.5". *Author's Collection. $10-15 each.*

Tico Toys altar boys, 1940s, not embossed. Silver flash, red flash, white, and blue plastic with red and flesh colored paint, 3.50" x 1.50". *Author's Collection. $8-10 each.*

Tico Toys altar boy, late 1940s, not embossed. Pink plastic with blue paint, 3.50" x 1.50". *Author's Collection. $8-10.*

Three Irwin altar boys on a tray with candle and a tree, late 1940s-1950s, embossed Irwin Plastics. White, red plastic with red, yellow, and black paint, 9" x 4.50". *(Angels and altar boys came in many different combinations on trays.) Author's Collection. $35-45*

Irwin angel on tray with tree, late 1940s-1950s, embossed Irwin Plastics. White and red plastic with gold paint, 4.50" x 3.50". *Author's Collection. $18-25.*

Irwin altar boy, late 1940s, embossed Irwin Plastics. White plastic with black and flesh colored paint, 3.75" x 1.75". *Courtesy of Bertram M. Choen, Irwin Plastics Corporation, Estate Collection. $10-18.*

Irwin angel hanging ornament, 1940s-1950s, embossed Irwin Plastics. White plastic with yellow paint, 4" x 3.50". *Courtesy of Bertram M. Cohen, Irwin Plastics Corporation Estate Collection.* $10-15.

Glo-rious Angel light by Glolite, early 1950s. Made in U.S.A. White plastic with silver flash, flesh, red, and blue paint, the box measures 9" x 10". *Author's Collection.* $35-55.

Large Angel light, 1980s, Union Products. Made in U.S.A. White plastic with gold, flesh color, yellow, blue, and red paint, 20" x 10". *Courtesy of Joy Pinegan.* $15-25.

Tico Toys Angel, late 1940s, not embossed. White plastic with gold paint, 4" x 3.50". *Author's Collection.* $12-20.

Tico Toys Angels, late 1940s, not embossed. Silver, flash with flesh colored and gold paint, 4" x 3.50". *Author's Collection. $12-20 each.*

Noma Tree Top Angel, 1950s, not embossed. Made in U.S.A. This Angel is a good addition to a Noma Light Collection. The Noma Light Company has made Christmas lights for over seventy-five years. White plastic with gold, red, blue, and yellow paint, 9" x 4.50". *Courtesy of Richard Miller. Photo by Richard Miller. $45-55.*

Above: Paramount Angel light, 1950s, not embossed. Made in U.S.A. White and clear plastic with gold, yellow, blue, black, and red paint, 9" x 9". *Author's Collection. $ 25-40.*

Right: Box for Paramount angel light. *Courtesy of Richard Miller.*

Angel, 1950s. Made in U.S.A. White plastic with blue, gold, red, and flesh paint. *Courtesy of Richard Miller. Photo by Richard Miller. $25-40.*

Royalite angel in original box, 1950s. White and clear plastic with gold, red, and blue paint. *Courtesy of Richard Miller. Photo by Richard Miller. $35-50.*

Angel, 1950s. Made in U.S.A. Painted gold, white, and flesh. *Courtesy of Richard Miller. Photo by Richard Miller. $25-40.*

Angel, 1950s. Made in U.S.A. White, clear and brown plastic 8". *Courtesy of Richard Miller. Photo by Richard Miller. $25-40.*

A Collection of Paramount Angel lights. *Courtesy of Richard Miller. Photo by Richard Miller.*

Small cherub baby rattle, 1950s not embossed. Made in U.S.A. Cream colored plastic with gold paint, 3" x 1.50". *Author's Collection. $15-22.*

Christmas Mouse light, 1950s. Made in U.S.A. White plastic with red and black paint, 22" tall. *Courtesy of Mark and Judy Craven. Photo by Mark Craven. $40-60.*

Santa candy container and ornament Irwin style, 1940s, not embossed. Made in U.S.A. White plastic with antique white paint, 4" x 2". Early Irwin can be unmarked. *Author's Collection. $20-35.*

Irwin Santa, 1950s, embossed Irwin Plastics.
Glowing pink plastic with white paint, 5" x 2.50".
Courtesy of Suzy and Dale Thomas. $20-35.

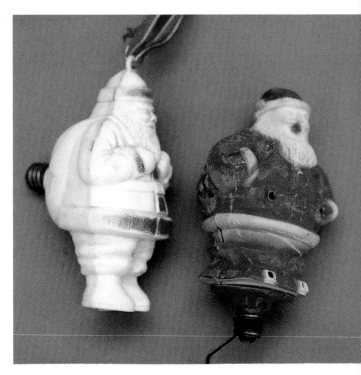

Santa lights, 1940s not embossed. Made in U.S.A. Red and white
plastic with red and white paint, 4" x 2.50". *Courtesy of Carol
Thompson. $15-20 each.*

Small Irwin Santa sleigh, candy container, 1950s, embossed Irwin Plastics.
White plastic with red paint, 3.50" x 2". *Author's Collection. $15-25.*

Santa,1940s. Inflammable celluloid. Irwin
Plastics Corporation Estate Collection.
Courtesy of Bertram M. Cohen. $85-100.

Easter and Christmas collectibles. Nonflammable celluloid, regular celluloid. Irwin Plastics Corporation Estate Collection. *Courtesy of Bertram M. Cohen. $45-100-85.*

Irwin Plastics Corporation estate Collection, 1930s-1940s. Celluloid hanging Santa ornament, 3.75" x 1.50". *Courtesy of Bertram M. Cohen. $45-65.*

Irwin Plastics Corporation Estate Collection, 1930s-1940s, celluloid and nonflammable celluloid Santas. L. 4" x 1.75", R. 4" x 1.75". *Courtesy of Bertram M. Cohen. $65- 100, each.*

Iwin Plastics Corp. Estate Collection, 1930s-1940s. Celluloid and nonflammable celluloid, hanging Santas. L. 3.50" x 2", R. 4" x 2.50". *Courtesy of Bertram M. Cohen. $45-65.*

Small Irwin Santa sleigh, candy container, 1950s, embossed Irwin Plastics. Silver and red flash paint, 3.50" x 2". *Courtesy of Suzy and Dale Thomas. $15-25.*

E. Rosen/Tico Toys deer on wheels, candy container, late 1940s-1950s, not embossed. Pink and yellow plastic with green paint, 5" x 5". *Author's Collection. $75-95.*

Irwin Plastics Corporation Estate Collection, 1930s-1940s, celluloid and nonflammable celluloid Santas. L. 7" x 2.50", R. 3" x 1". *Courtesy of Bertram M. Cohen. $65-100, each.*

E. Rosen/Tico Toys deer on wheels candy container, late 1940s-1950s, not embossed. Pink and yellow plastic with blue paint, 5" x 5". *Author's Collection. $75-95.*

Rudolph the Red Nose Reindeer light up pins, late 1940s-1950s.
Made in U.S.A. White and cream-colored plastic with green,
brown, and black paint, L. 3.50" x 1.75", R. 2.50" x 3". *Author's
Collection*. $25-35 each.

Irwin Plastics reindeers, late 1940s, not embossed. White plastic
with red paint. These reindeer can be found on platforms with trees.
Large deer 4.50" x 5", small deer are 2.50" x 3". *Courtesy of Suzy and
Dale Thomas*. Large $15-20, small $8-10.

Santa and Rudolph light up pins, late 1940s-1950s. Made in U.S.A. White plastic with brown, blue, red, flesh
color, black, and gold paint, the noses light up when you pull the bell. Santas 2" x 1.50", Rudolph 2.25" x 2.50".
Author's Collection. $20-35 each.

Above: E. Rosen Reindeer Comet and Cupid, candy containers, rare, late 1940s-1950s, not embossed. Original childhood toy of Suzy Thomas. *$25-40, each.*

Right: Original Reindeer tags from E. Rosen Company.

Santa and Rudolph flasher eyes cups, 1950s, not embossed. Made in U.S.A. by Eagle Company. White plastic with brown and red paint, 5" x 3.5". *Courtesy of Suzy and Dale Thomas. $15-20 each.*

Rudolph with small Irwin reindeer, rare. The small reindeer measures 3" x 2". *Courtesy of Suzy and Dale Thomas. $10, small reindeer.*

Rudolph the Red Nose Reindeer children's iron, early 1950s, embossed E. J. Kahn Company Chicago, Illinois. Cream colored plastic with brown, green and red paint with a metal base, 5" x 4". *Author's Collection. $55-75.*

Hard plastic reindeer made for an outdoor sleigh, 1950s and made for many years later to be manufactured out of vinyl. Cream colored plastic with brown, black, red and white paint, 13.5" x 9". *Author's Collection. $15-25.*

Rudolph the Red Nose Reindeer music box light, 1940s-1950s, manufactured by Ray Lite Electric Corp. New York City. Cream color and maroon plastic with brown, black, white and blue paint. His nose lights up, 8" x 7.5". *Author's Collection. $100-125.*

1960s deer, embossed. Made in Hong Kong deer. Cream colored plastic with brown and black paint, good quality plastic deer, 7" x 6". *Author's Collection. $10.*

Rudolph hanging ornaments, 1940s-1950s . Made in U.S.A., embossed Rudolph. Cream colored plastic with red, green, brown and black paint, 4" x 2.50". *Author's Collection. $15-25, each.*

Holiday pins, 1950s. Made in U.S.A. Green and red plastic with blue, red, green and yellow paint; the bells have holly berries inside, 2" x 1", the stocking is 2.50" x 1". *Author's Collection. $15-20 each.*

King Santa with shovel light, 1950s, embossed Harett-Gilmar Inc., New York City. Red, white and green plastic with black and red paint, the box is 10" x 10". *Author's Collection. $40-50.*

1960s hard plastic Bambi type deer, not embossed. Made in U.S.A. White plastic with brown, blue, black and white paint, L. 6" x 6", R. 6" x 4". *Author's Collection. $10 each.*

King Santa bank light holding Christmas tree, 1950s, embossed Harret-Gilmar Inc., New York City. Red plastic with white, flesh color and blue paint, 7" x 4". *Author's Collection.* $55-70.

King Santa bank light holding Christmas tree, 1950s, embossed Harett-Gilmar Inc., New York City. White plastic with red and blue paint/ original box, 7" x 4". *Author's Collection.* $65-85.

Santa window light, 1950s, not embossed. Made in U.S.A. Plastic front and metal back, white plastic with red, blue and flesh color paint, 8.50" x 3.75". *Author's Collection.* $35-50.

Santa window light, 1950s, not embossed. Made in U.S.A., flocked velvet body. White plastic with white, blue, red and flesh color paint, 8.50" x 3.75". *Courtesy of Carol Thompson.* $35-50.

King Santa Shootin' Sheriff bank, holding a gun, 1950s, embossed Harret-Gilmar Inc., New York City. White plastic with blue, red, and flesh colored paint, 7" x 4". *Author's Collection. $65-85.*

Halloween King Santa Cap'n Kid bank, holding a sword, 1950s, embossed Harret-Gilmar Inc., New York City. Red plastic with black, white and flesh color paint, 7" x 4". *Author's Collection. $85-125.*

King Santa Snowman bank, holding a shovel, 1950s, embossed Harret-Gilmar Inc., New York City. White and green plastic with black and red paint, 7" x 4". *Author's Collection. $55-70.*

Large plastic window Santa, 1940s-1950s, not embossed. Made in U.S.A. Red plastic with white, yellow, green, black, blue and flesh color paint, 32" x 12". *Courtesy of Carol Thompson. $85-125.*

Santa light, 1940s-1950s, embossed, General Prod. Co. Inc.
Providence, Rhode Island. Red and white plastic with black and
flesh color paint, 8" x 6". *Author's Collection. $55-70.*

Snowman carrying Christmas tree, 1940s-1950s, a Royalite Jolly
Christmas Character, Royal Electric Company, Pawtucket, Rhode
Island. White, green and black plastic with red and black paint,
7.50" x 5". *Author's Collection. $45-55.*

Jolly Christmas Characters' box, #948, original price $1.89. Box
measures 7.50" x 5". *Courtesy of Carol Thompson. $15.*

Santa holding bubble light, 1940s-1950s, a Royalite Jolly
Christmas Character, Royal Electric Company, Pawtucket,
Rhode Island. Red and white plastic with black and flesh
color paint, 7.50" x 5". *Author's Collection. $45-55*

Waving Santa light. Made in U.S.A. 1950s. White plastic with blue, red and flesh paint, 10" tall. *Courtesy of Richard Miller, Photo by Richard Miller. $45-60.*

Santa holding candy cane light, 1950s, embossed H. Y.-G.Prod. Co. Los Angeles, California #611. White and red plastic with black, red and flesh color paint, 8.50" x 5". *Courtesy of Carol Thompson. $35-55.*

1950s nonflammable celluloid hanging tree ornaments, 4" x 2". *Author's Collection. $5-8 each.*

1950s nonflammable celluloid Santa window head, 10" x 10". *Courtesy of Carol Thompson. $15-20.*

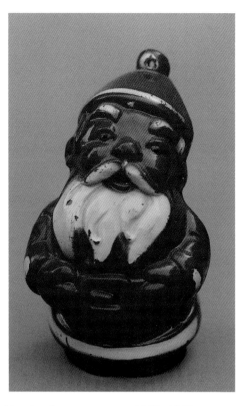

Hanging Santa ornament, not embossed. Made in U.S.A. 1950s. Red plastic with white, blue and flesh paint, 3.5" by 1". *Author's Collection. $15-25.*

Hanging Santa ornament, 1940s-1950s, not embossed. Made in U.S.A. Red plastic with white and black paint, rare, 3" x 2". *Author's Collection. $20-35.*

Santa indoor light, 1950s, Judith Novelty Company. White plastic with red, antique white, blue, black and flesh color paint, 16" x 7". He was made into the 1960s. *Author's Collection. $45-65.*

Above: Bird tree lights, 1950s, not embossed. Made in U.S.A. Red and yellow plastic with black paint, 4.50" x 3". *Author's Collection. $10-15 each.*

Left: Santa window light, 1950s, not embossed. Made in U.S.A. White plastic with green, red and blue paint, beautiful face, 15" x 13". *Author's Collection. $55-75.*

Sterling candolier window decoration. Made in U.S.A. *Author's Collection. $15-35.*

Large indoor candle, late 1940s-1950s . Made in U.S.A. 18" x 4". *Author's Collection. $25-40.*

1950s Christmas tree salt and peppers in original box. Box is 12.50" x 4". *Author's Collection. $20-35.*

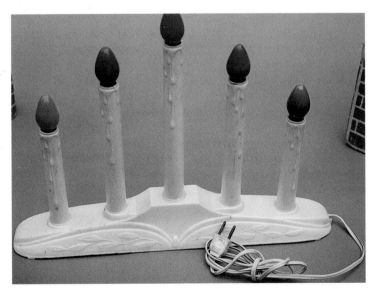

Royalite Indoor candle lights, 1940s-1950s, not embossed. Made in U.S.A. Cream color plastic. *Author's Collection. $15-35 for six candles.*

1960s hard plastic and vinyl Christmas bells, not embossed. Made in U.S.A. Red plastic with vinyl poinsettia. *Author's Collection.* $10.

1960s Santa, candy container. Made in Hong Kong. Red and clear plastic with yellow, black, gold, blue, white, red and flesh color paint, 4" x 2", with original candy. *Author's Collection.* $20-35.

Christmas tree, battery operated blinking light, 1960s. Made in Japan. Red and white plastic with green plastic tree, patent #442526. Box measures 6.50" x 2.75". *Author's Collection.* $25-40.

1960s battery operated candlelight, embossed. Made in Hong Kong. Clear, green and red plastic with vinyl holly berries, 6" x 6". *Author's Collection.* $15-25.

1960s Santa candy container. Made in Hong Kong. During the 1960s this type of hard plastic Santa became rare. Almost all types of candy containers were beginning to be made of vinyl. White and red plastic with yellow, green, black, gold, red and flesh color paint, 5.50" x 3". He comes apart in the middle. *Author's Collection. $25-40.*

1960s hard plastic Christmas card box, made in Hong Kong. Red and cream color plastic with white, green, blue and gold paint, 10" x 10". It folds in and out. *Author's Collection. $20-35.*

Along with the Christmas novelties shown above, the same company manufactured this 1960s hard plastic Easter card box, made in Hong Kong. Yellow plastic with white, blue, red, green and black paint, 10" x 7". It folds in and out. *Courtesy of Dave and Ginny Wellington. $20-35.*

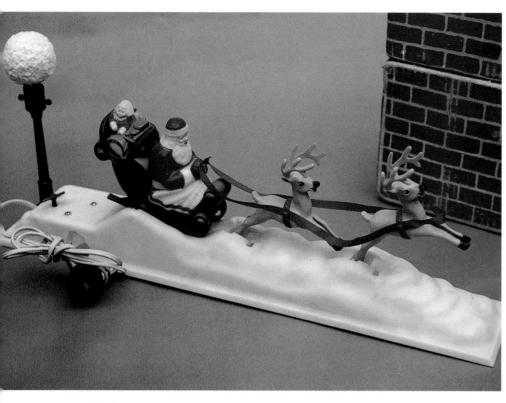

1960s Santa elf light cover, not embossed. Red, white and black plastic with black and flesh color paint, 4.50" x 2.50". *Author's Collection. $10-15.*

1960s Santa in sleigh, musical, animated light, made in Hong Kong. White, tan and green plastic with red, yellow, blue, tan, white and flesh color paint, 12" x 3". *Author's Collection. $25-45.*

1960s holiday pins, both are animated. Made in Hong Kong. *Author's Collection. $10 each.*

1960s cake top Santa head, $12-15.

Newer cup cake hard plastic sticks, 1980s, not embossed. Each one measures approximately 1.50" x 1". White, red and green plastic with green, gold and red paint. *Author's Collection. $1 each.*

1960s reindeer plant decorations. Made in Japan. The heads measure 1.50" x 1". *Author's Collection. $2 each.*

1960s hanging tree ornament with plastic and vinyl scene inside. 4" x 2". *Author's Collection. $ 3-5 each.*

1960s vinyl filled Santa candy containers. Made in Hong Kong. Green and red vinyl, the heads come off to put candy inside, 3.50" x 1.50". *Author's Collection. $3-5 each.*

Early 1960s figural Santa snow dome. Made in Hong Kong for Brite Star Manufacturing Co., Philadelphia Pa. Red, black and clear plastic with white, black, blue, antique white and flesh color paint, 6" x 3". *Author's Collection. $35-55.*

Early 1960s figural Snowman snow dome. Made in Hong Kong for Brite Star Manufacturing Co. Philadelphia, Pa. White, black, clear blue and clear plastic with green, red, blue and black paint, 6" x 3". *Author's Collection. $ 35-55.*

1990s figural Snowman snow dome, made in China. White, black and clear plastic with red, green, yellow and blue paint, 5.50" x 3". *Author's Collection. $8-10.*

Fun World Snowman wind-up walker, 1990s made in China. White and black plastic with green, black and red paint, 3.50" x 2". *Author's Collection. $5-10.*

1960s stylized Snowman, not embossed, . Made in U.S.A. White, red and black plastic with black paint, 3.50" x 2.50". *Author's Collection. $8-10.*

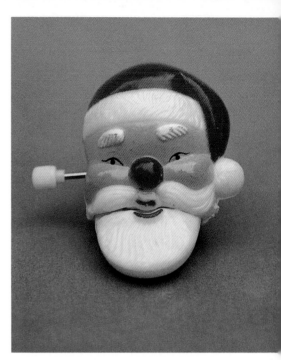

1960s figural Santa snow domes. Made in Hong Kong. Red, black, white and clear plastic with brown, black and flesh color paint, L. 5.50" x 3.75" #8824, R 3.875" x 3" #8820. *Courtesy of Carol Thompson. $35-50 each.*

Santa Wind-up head, 1990s. Made in China. White plastic with blue, red and flesh color paint. When you wind him up his mouth opens and closes, 1.50" x 1.50". *Author's Collection. $5-8.*

1960s push button Santa puppet. Made in Hong Kong for Kohner Bros. Inc., E. Paterson, New Jersey. Green and red plastic with black, white and flesh color paint, 3.75" x 2.50". *Courtesy of Carol Thompson. $20-35.*

Marx Toys wind-up Santa vibrator doll. Made in Japan, 1968. White and black plastic with red and flesh paint, 4.50" x 2.50". *Courtesy of Carol Thompson. $20-35.*

Santa Rolly Poly with bell inside, embossed Kiddie Productions Inc. , Avon, Massachusetts 02332, 1980s. Red and white plastic with blue and flesh paint, 4.50" x 3". *Courtesy of Carol Thompson.* $10-15.

Santa friction toy, 1960s. Made in Hong Kong for Fun World Inc. Red and white plastic with black, blue, red, yellow and flesh color paint, 3.75" x 2.50". *Courtesy of Carol Thompson.* $25-40.

Above: Rolly Poly Santa with bell, 1960s, not embossed. Probably made in Hong Kong. Red and white plastic with black, yellow, blue, white and flesh paint, 8" x 5". *Courtesy of Carol Thompson.* $25-40.

Right: Union Products Snowman light, 1980s. White plastic with red, green and black paint, 12" x 7". *Author's Collection.* $10-15.

1980s hard plastic stocking holders. Made in China. Red, white, black and yellow plastic with green, yellow, brown, black, red and flesh color paint, 7" x 4". *Author's Collection. $5 each.*

1960s Snowman musical head. Made in Hong Kong. White and black plastic with red, green, brown and black paint, 9" x 5.5". *Author's Collection. $25-40.*

Mr. And Mrs. Claus cake top decoration, 1960s. Made in Hong Kong. 3" x 3". *Author's Collection. $3-5.*

Rocking Santa. Made in Hong Kong, early 1960s. Brown, red and white plastic with black, white, red, gray and flesh paint, 8" by 4". *Author's Collection. $20-35.*

European Santa elf doll, with plastic face,1940s-1950s . *Courtesy of Carol Thompson. $45-65.*

A Collection of vinyl and plastic face Santas, 1950s-1960s. *Courtesy of Carol Thompson.*

EASTER

Irwin rabbit with magician hat. The tail is spring loaded, 1950s, embossed Irwin Plastics. Yellow and black plastic with red, white and black paint, 9.50" x 4". *Courtesy of Bertram M. Cohen, Irwin Plastics Corporation Estate Collection. $65-85.*

Irwin runny bunny, mechanical, 1950s, embossed Irwin Plastics. Yellow plastic with red paint in violet cloth rompers, 7" x 5.50", with original Gimbels price tag. *Courtesy of Bertram M. Cohen, Irwin Plastics Corporation Estate Collection. $65-95.*

Irwin leaping lamb, 1950s, embossed Irwin Plastics. White, green and yellow plastic with yellow paint, the lamb is on a spring and rock back and forth, 4.75" x 3.50". *Courtesy of Bertram M. Cohen, Irwin Plastics Corporation Estate Collection. $45-65.*

Irwin singing mechanical bird, 1950s, embossed Irwin Plastics. Yellow and black plastic with red, black and white paint, 5.50" x 5", original box. *Courtesy of Bertram M. Cohen, Irwin Plastics Corporation Estate Collection. $75-95.*

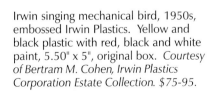

Irwin nodder bunny with glasses, Yellow plastic with pink paint and black plastic glasses. 6" by 3.75". *Courtesy of Mark and Judy Craven, Photo by Mark Craven.* $35-55.

Irwin nodder bunny with basket, 1950s, embossed Irwin Plastics. Yellow plastic with red paint, 6" x 3.75". *Author's Collection.* $35-50.

Above: Irwin rooster with egg on platform, 1950s, embossed Irwin Plastics. Green, yellow and clear plastic with red paint, 4" x 3.75". *Courtesy of Dave and Ginny Wellington.* $30-45.

Left: Irwin boy rabbit rattle, 1950s, embossed Irwin Plastics. Yellow plastic with red paint, 6" x 2.50". *Courtesy of Bertram M. Cohen, Irwin Plastics CorporationEstate Collection.* $25-35.

Irwin bunny with wheelbarrow candy container, 1950s, embossed Irwin Plastics. Pink, yellow and red plastic with blue paint, 5" x 6". *Courtesy of Suzy and Dale Thomas. $45-65.*

Irwin bunny with wheelbarrow and glasses candy container, 1950s, embossed Irwin Plastics. Yellow, blue and black plastic with purple and white paint, 5" x 6". *Courtesy of Bertram M. Cohen, Irwin Plastics Corporation Estate Collection. $55-75.*

Irwin bunny with wheelbarrow, candy container, 1950s, embossed Irwin Plastics. White, green and yellow plastic with pink and black paint, 5" x 6". *Author's Collection $35-45, bunny is faded.*

Irwin bunny with wheelbarrow and tools, candy container, 1950s, embossed Irwin Plastics. Pink, blue and yellow plastic with blue and yellow paint, tools are not original, 5" x 6". *Courtesy of Suzy and Dale Thomas. $45-65, tools $15-18.*

Irwin rooster rattle, 1950s, embossed Irwin Plastics. Yellow plastic with red paint, 3.50" x 2.50". *Author's Collection.* $15-25.

Irwin rooster, 1950s, embossed Irwin Plastics. Yellow plastic with blue and red paint, 3.50" x 2.50", rattle. *Courtesy of Richard Miller, Photo by Richard Miller.* $15-25.

Irwin rooster rattle, 1950s, embossed Irwin Plastics. Green plastic with red paint, 3.50" x 2.50". *Author's Collection.* $15-25.

Irwin small bunnies with carrot, candy containers, 1950s, embossed Irwin Plastics. Clear green, clear white plastic with yellow and red paint and sparkles, 4" x 2". *Courtesy of Suzy and Dale Thomas.* $20-35 each.

Irwin small bunny with carrot rattle, 1950s, embossed Irwin Plastics. Yellow plastic with blue and red paint, 4" x 2". *Author's Collection.* $15-25.

Irwin small bunny with carrot rattle, 1950s, embossed Irwin Plastics. Pink plastic with blue paint, 4" x 2". *Author's Collection. $20-35.*

Irwin bunny, 1950s, embossed Irwin Plastics. Flash gold and red paint, 6" x 2". *Courtesy of Bertram M. Cohen, Irwin Plastics Corporation Estate Collection. $25-45.*

Irwin bunny, 1950s, embossed Irwin Plastics. Clear pink plastic candy container, 6" x 2". *Courtesy of Bertram M. Cohen, Irwin Plastics Corporation Estate Collection. $25-45.*

Irwin girl bunny, rattle,1950s, embossed Irwin Plastics. Yellow plastic, 5" x 2.50". *Courtesy of Bert Cohen, Irwin Plastics Corporation Estate Collection. $20-35.*

Irwin Plastics Corporation Estate Collection, bunny, chick and egg rocker, and Bunny pulling egg cart, 1930s-1940s celluloid and nonflammable celluloid. *Courtesy of Bertram M. Cohen. L $85-100, R. $55-75.*

Irwin Plastics Corporation Estate Collection Swan with Rabbit, 1930s-1940s nonflammable celluloid. *Courtesy of Bertram M. Cohen. $125-150.*

Irwin Plastics Corporation Estate Collection Duck dressed in jacket and purple hat, 1930s-1940s, nonflammable celluloid. *Courtesy of Bertram M. Cohen. $45-55.*

Irwin Plastics Corporation Estate Collection Duck in suit and hat, 1930s-1940s nonflammable celluloid. *Courtesy of Bertram M. Cohen. $55-75.*

Irwin Plastics Corporation Estate Collection Chick in suit with top hat, 1930s-1940s, nonflammable celluloid. *Courtesy of Bertram M. Cohen. $55-75.*

Irwin Plastics Corporation Estate Collection Bunny in clown outfit, 1930s-1940s nonflammable celluloid. *Courtesy of Bertram M. Cohen. $65-85.*

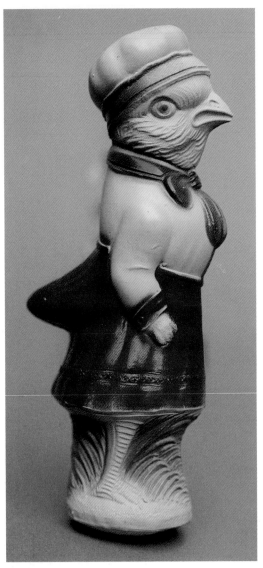

Irwin Plastics Corporation Estate Collection Rooster pulling cart with Rabbit and eggs, 1930s-1940s, nonflammable celluloid. *Courtesy of Bertram M. Cohen.* $65-85.

Irwin Plastics Corporation Estate Collection Chick in dress and hat, 1930s-1940s non-flammable celluloid. *Courtesy of Bertram M. Cohen.* $65-85.

Above: Irwin Plastics Corporation Estate Collection. Bunny golfer dressed in jacket, pant and scarf, 1930s-1940s nonflammable celluloid. *Courtesy of Bertram M. Cohen.* $85-100.

Left: Irwin Plastics CorporationEstate Collection Rabbit with basket on wheel platform, 1930s-1940s, nonflammable celluloid. *Courtesy of Bertram M. Cohen.* $100-125.

Irwin Plastics Corporation Estate Collection, celluloid Duck, bath tub rattle, 1930s. *Courtesy of Bertram M. Cohen. $55-65.*

Irwin Plastics Corporation Estate Collection Bath Tub Duck, 1950s. Red plastic with yellow and black paint, 4" x 3.50". *Courtesy of Bertram M. Cohen. $20-35.*

Irwin Plastics Corporation Estate Collection, celluloid, Bath Tub Swan rattle, 1930s. *Courtesy of Bertram M. Cohen. $40-55.*

Irwin Clear Bunny candy container, 1950s, embossed Irwin Plastics. Clear plastic with red and white paint, 8" x 3.50". *Courtesy of Bertram M. Cohen. $45-65, glasses are missing.*

E. Rosen Bunny with egg candy container, 1950s, not embossed. Yellow plastic with green paint, 4" x 2". *Author's Collection. $18-25.*

E. Rosen Bunny with egg candy container, 1950s, not embossed. Yellow plastic with green, pink, purple, and black paint, 4" x 2". *Author's Collection. $18-25.*

E. Rosen Bunny with egg candy container, 1950s, not embossed. Yellow and pink plastic with green paint, original floral arch from Pawtucket, Providence, Rhode Island novelty area. *Author's Collection. $25-55, rare.*

E. Rosen Bunny with apron and hat candy container, 1950s, not embossed. Yellow plastic with green, purple, red and white paint, 6" x 3". *Author's Collection. $40-65.*

E. Rosen bunny with egg candy containers, 1950s, original box. *Courtesy of Mark and Judy Craven, Photo by Mark Craven. $135-150.*

E. Rosen Bunnies in car, candy container, 1950s, embossed Rosbro Plastics. Yellow, green and pink plastic with blue and green plastic, 7.50" x 3.50" x 5". *Courtesy of Richard Miller, Photo by Richard Miller. $125-165.*

E. Rosen Bunny in car candy container, 1950s, car is embossed Rosbro Plastics. Pink, green and yellow plastic with green paint, the car is 7.50" x 3.50". *Courtesy of Richard Miller, Photo by Richard Miller. $95-125.*

E. Rosen bunny in car candy container, 1950s, not embossed. Pink, yellow and purple plastic with green and black paint. 4.5" by 5", rare. *Courtesy of Mark and Judy Craven, Photo by Mark Craven. $185-200.*

E. Rosen bunnies in Model T Car, candy container, 1950s, embossed Rosbro plastics. Pink, green and yellow plastic with blue, red and green paint. Original "Happy Easter" sign. 6.5" by 3" by 6". *Courtesy of Mark and Judy Craven, Photo by Mark Craven.* $150-175

E. Rosen Bunnies in Model T Car, candy container, 1950s, embossed Rosbro Plastics. Pink, green, and yellow plastic with blue, red and green paint, 6.50" x 3" x 6". *Courtesy of Richard Miller, Photo by Richard Miller.* $125-150.

E. Rosen Easter Canoe candy container, 1950s, not embossed. Pink and white plastic with green and yellow paint. 3" by 2" *Courtesy of Mark and Judy Craven, Photo by Mark Craven.* $45-65.

E. Rosen bunnies riding piggyback candy container, 1950s not embossed. Pink and yellow plastic with green paint 4.5" by 4.5". *Courtesy of Mark and Judy Craven, Photo by Mark Craven.* $45-75.

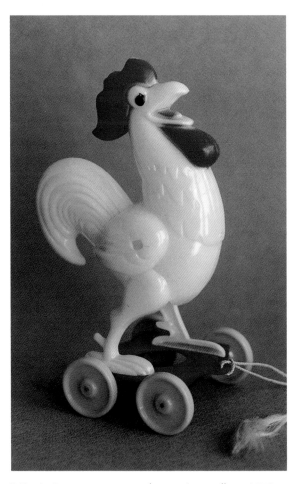

E. Rosen Rooster pulling Duck in cart, candy container, 1950s, not embossed. Yellow, green, pink and blue plastic with red, black and green paint, 8" x 9". *Courtesy of Dave and Ginny Wellington. $85-100.*

E. Rosen Rooster on cart candy container pull toy, 1950s, not embossed. Green, red and yellow plastic with black red paint, original tassel, 8" x 5". *Courtesy of Dave and Ginny Wellington. $55-65.*

E. Rosen Rooster pulling Bunny in cart, candy container, 1950s, not embossed. Pink, yellow and green plastic with red, blue and black paint, 6.50" x 6.50. *Courtesy of Richard Miller, Photo by Richard Miller. $55-75.*

E. Rosen Bunny with rake candy container, 1950s, not embossed. Yellow plastic with blue paint, 4" x 1.75". *Courtesy of Suzy and Dale Thomas $35-45.*

E. Rosen Bunny with missing tool candy container, 1950s, not embossed. Yellow plastic with red paint, 4" x 1.75". *Author's Collection $18-20.*

E. Rosen Rooster pulling Bunny in cart with rake, candy container, 1950s, not embossed, Easter Express. Yellow, green and red plastic with blue, red and black paint, 6" x 6" x 3". *Courtesy of Suzy and Dale Thomas. $85-100.*

E. Rosen bunny with egg in cart, candy container,1950s not embossed. Red, yellow and green plastic with red, black and blue paint, 4.5" by 6". Courtesy *of Richard Miller, Photo by Richard Miller. $50-65.*

E. Rosen Lamb pulling golf Bunny in cart, candy container,1950s, not embossed. The Rosen Lamb faces sideways. The Irwin Lamb faces front. Pink, green, and yellow plastic with green and black paint, 6" x 3.50". *Courtesy of Suzy and Dale Thomas. $45-65.*

E. Rosen bunny with egg and hat on platform, candy container, 1950s , not embossed. Green, yellow, pink and red plastic with red and blue paint. 3.5" by 4.75". *Courtesy of Mark and Judy Craven, Photo by Mark Craven. $45-55.*

E. Rosen Bunny pushing baby carriage candy container, 1950s, not embossed. Yellow and green plastic with blue and red paint, 9" x 8.50". *Author's Collection. $175-200*

Tico Toys Bunny bank candy container, late 1940s not embossed. Pink plastic with blue and red paint, 12" x 5". *Author's Collection. $125-150.*

E. Rosen Bunny pushing baby carriage candy container, 1950s, not embossed. Green and pink plastic with blue and red paint, 9" x 8.50". *Courtesy of Richard Miller, Photo by Richard Miller. $175-200*

E. Rosen Bunny pushing baby carriage candy container, 1950s, not embossed. Pink and yellow plastic with green paint, 9" by 8.50". *Courtesy of Richard Miller, Photo By Richard Miller. $175-200*

Tico Toys Jolly Duck pull toy bank, late 1940s, not embossed. White and red plastic with yellow and red paint, 6" by 10". *Courtesy of Richard Miller. Photo by Richard Miller. $200-275.*

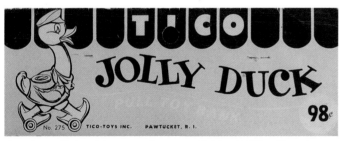

Tico Toys Jolly Duck bag top. *Courtesy of Richard Miller. Photo by Richard Miller.*

Tico Toys Bunny bank candy container, late 1940s, not embossed. Yellow plastic with blue and white paint, 12" x 10". *Author's Collection. $200-275. This is the same mold as large Halloween clown.*

E. Rosen long eared Bunny on wheels pushing wheelbarrow, candy container, wheelbarrow is embossed Rosbro Plastics, late 1940s-1950s. Pink, blue, green, and yellow plastic with red and white paint, 6" x 7". *Courtesy of Suzy and Dale Thomas. $65-85.*

Three different colored E. Rosen long eared Bunnies with wheelbarrow candy containers. The wheelbarrow is embossed Rosbro Plastics. The bunny is not embossed, 1940s-1950s. Yellow, pink, white, and green plastic with green, red, and white paint, 6" x 5.50". *Courtesy of Richard Miller. Photo by Richard Miller. $45-60 each.*

E. Rosen long eared Bunny on wheels, late 1940s-1950s, not embossed. Yellow, green, and white plastic with red and blue paint, wheelbarrow is missing, although he could have been sold without it, 7" x 3". *Courtesy of Richard Miller. Photo by Richard Miller. $35-45.*

E. Rosen long eared Bunny on wheels with glasses candy container, late 1940s-1950s, not embossed, he never had a wheelbarrow, his hands are filled in. Yellow, green and black plastic with red and white paint, 7" x 3". *Courtesy of Suzy and Dale Thomas. $65-85.*

E. Rosen long eared Bunny on wheels with wheelbarrow candy container, late 1940s-1950s, the wheelbarrow is embossed Rosbro Plastics. Red, yellow, green, white, and black plastic, 6" x 7". *Courtesy of Suzy and Dale Thomas. $65-85.*

E. Rosen long eared Bunny riding tricycle cart, candy container, late 1940s-1950s, not embossed, he is carrying an E. Rosen surprise egg. Pink, yellow and green plastic with red and white paint, 7" x 7". *Author's Collection. $95-115.*

E. Rosen long eared bunny riding tricycle cart, candy container, late 1940s-1950s, not embossed. Pink, green and yellow plastic with red paint, 7" by 7". Courtesy of *Mark and Judy Craven. Photo by Mark Craven. $95-115.*

E. Rosen long eared Bunny with wheelbarrow candy container, late 1940s-1950s, the wheelbarrow is embossed Rosbro Plastics. Yellow and blue plastic with red and white paint, 6" x 6". *Author's Collection. $45-65.*

E. Rosen long eared Bunny with wheelbarrow candy container, late 1940s-1950s, wheelbarrow is embossed Rosbro Plastics. Purple, blue and yellow plastic with white and red paint, 6" x 6". *Author's Collection. $45-65.*

Two pink E. Rosen small Bunny candy containers, late 1940s-1950s, not embossed. Pink plastic with black paint, 4" x 2". *Author's Collection.* $20-30.

E. Rosen small Bunny candy container, late 1940s-1950s, not embossed. Pink and yellow plastic with blue paint, 4" x 2". *Courtesy of Suzy and Dale Thomas.* $25-35.

E. Rosen Duck candy container, late 1940s-1950s, not embossed. Pink plastic with blue paint, 4" x 2.50". *Author's Collection.* $25-35 each.

E. Rosen Duck whistle candy containers, late 1940s-1950s, not embossed. White plastic with yellow and red paint, 4" x 2.50". *Courtesy of Suzy and Dale Thomas.* $25-35 each.

E. Rosen Cowboy Duck on wheels, with original tassel candy container (he is missing one gun), late 1940s-1950s, not embossed. Green, yellow, and blue plastic with red and green paint, 4.50" x 2.75". *Author's Collection. $45-65.*

E. Rosen duck with hat and original tassel on wheels candy container, late 1940s-1950s, not embossed. Green and yellow plastic with red and green paint, 4.5" by 2.75". *Courtesy of Mark and Judy Craven. Photo by Mark Craven. $45-65.*

E. Rosen duck on wheels napkin holder/ candy container, 1940s-1950s, not embossed. Pink, green and yellow plastic with red paint. *Courtesy of Mark and Judy Craven. Photo by Mark Craven. $45-65.*

1960s Duck and Chick rattles. Blue plastic with red paint, L.- made in U.S.A., 2" x 1.50"; R.- made in Hong Kong, 4" x 2.50". *Author's Collection.* L. $3-5, R. $10-15.

E. Rosen Duck whistle candy container, late 1940s-1950s, not embossed. Pink plastic with green paint, 4" x 2". *Author's Collection. $25-35.*

E. Rosen Bunny with television camera candy container, late 1940s-1950s, not embossed. Pink and yellow plastic with green paint, 5" x 3". *Courtesy of Suzy and Dale Thomas.* $65-95.

E. Rosen bunny riding rocket candy container, late 1940s-1950s not embossed. Yellow plastic with green paint, 4" by 2". *Courtesy of Mark and Judy Craven. Photo by Mark Craven.* $55-75.

E. Rosen Bunny riding rocket candy container, late 1940s-1950s, not embossed. Red and pink plastic with blue paint, 4" x 2". *Courtesy of Suzy and Dale Thomas.* $55-75.

Above: E. Rosen Bunnies riding rockets candy container, late 1940s-1950s, not embossed. Yellow and red plastic with green paint, 4" x 2". *Author's Collection.* $55-75 each.

Left: Duck on egg, hard plastic candy container, 1960s, not embossed, exceptional piece. Made in Japan, 7" tall. *Courtesy of Mark and Judy Craven. Photo by Mark Craven.* $125-150.

E. Rosen Duck on jet candy container, late 1940s-1950s, not embossed. Yellow and pink plastic with blue paint, 4" by 2". *Author's Collection. $55-75.*

E. Rosen Bunny on wheels candy container, 1950s, embossed Rosbro Plastics, this Bunny was later made of vinyl. Pink, green, and yellow plastic with purple and white paint, with original tassel, 5" x 2.50". *Author's Collection. $45-65.*

E. Rosen Duck on jet candy container, late 1940s-1950s, not embossed. Pink and yellow plastic with blue paint, 4" by 2". *Courtesy of Mark and Judy Craven. Photo by Mark Craven. $55-75.*

E. Rosen Bunny on wheels candy container, 1950s, embossed Rosbro plastics. Yellow and green plastic with black paint, 5" x 2.5". *Courtesy of Mark and Judy Craven, Photo by Mark Craven. $45-65*

E. Rosen Bunny on wheels candy container, 1950s, embossed Rosbro Plastics. Purple, yellow, and green plastic with black paint, 5" x 2.50". *Courtesy of Suzy and Dale Thomas. $45-65.*

E. Rosen Boy and Girl Chick candy containers, 1950s, not embossed. Pink and yellow plastic with red and green paint, 4" x 1.50". *Author's Collection. $25-35 each.*

E. Rosen Boy and Girl Chick candy containers, 1950s, not embossed. Yellow plastic with red and pink paint, 4" x 1.50". *Courtesy of Suzy and Dale Thomas. $25-35 each.*

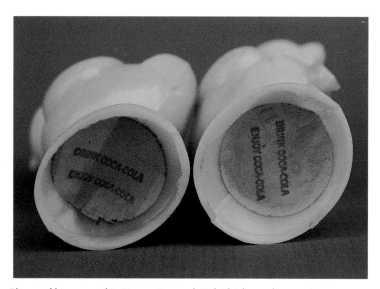

Photo of bottoms of E. Rosen Boy and Girl Chick candy containers, advertisement for Coca Cola. *Courtesy of Suzy and Dale Thomas.*

E. Rosen small Duck and Rooster candy containers, 1950s, not embossed. Pink and white plastic with red and green paint, the Duck was holding something in his hands, 3" x 1.50". *Courtesy of Suzy and Dale Thomas. $15-25 each.*

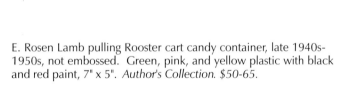

E. Rosen Lamb candy container, late 1940s-1950s, not embossed. Yellow plastic with blue paint, 3" x 3". *Courtesy of Suzy and Dale Thomas. $20-35.*

E. Rosen Lamb pulling Rooster cart candy container, late 1940s-1950s, not embossed. Green, pink, and yellow plastic with black and red paint, 7" x 5". *Author's Collection. $50-65.*

E. Rosen Lamb pulling wagon Easter Express candy container with three Knickerbocker hitchhikers, late 1940s-1950s, not embossed. Pink, green, and yellow plastic with black and green paint, 8" x 3.50". *Courtesy of Suzy and Dale Thomas. $50-65.*

E. Rosen/Tico Toys sucker holders, late 1940s-1950s, not embossed. Yellow and pink plastic with purple, red and green paint. The E. Rosen shovel in the middle measures 7" x 2", the two Tico Toy holders on each side measure 4.50" x 2". *Courtesy of Richard Miller, Photo by Richard Miller. $18-25 each.*

E. Rosen duck shovel sucker holder, late 1940s-1950s not embossed. Pink plastic with blue paint, 7" by 2". *Courtesy of Mark and Judy Craven, Photo by Mark Craven. $18-25.*

E. Rosen Chick on tricycle sucker holder, late 1940s-1950s, not embossed. Pink plastic with green paint, 4.50" x 2". *Author's Collection. $18-25.*

Original Tico Toys bag showing Chick on tricycle, 1940s. *Courtesy of Dave and Ginny Wellington. $45-65.*

85

Tico Toys/E. Rosen Goosey Gander and Little Boy Blue sucker holders, late 1940s-1950s, not embossed. White plastic with blue and green paint, L. 4.50" x 3", R. 5" x 2.50". *Author's Collection. $18-25 each.*

Tico Toys/E. Rosen Goosey Gander sucker holder, 1940s-1950s, not embossed. Yellow plastic with red paint, 4.50" x 3". *Author's Collection. $18-25.*

E. Rosen bunny with drum sucker holder, 1940s-1950s not embossed. Yellow plastic with red paint, 4.5" by 2.5". *Courtesy of Mark and Judy Craven, Photo by Mark Craven. $18-25.*

Tico Toys Engine candy container, 1940s not embossed. Pink and yellow plastic with green and yellow paint, 7" x 4.50". *Author's Collection. $125-175.*

Bunny artist egg cup, 1950s. Made in U.S.A. White, red, and green plastic with brown, yellow, blue, and red paint, 3.50" x 1.50". *Courtesy of Richard Miller, Photo by Richard Miller. $35-45.*

Tico Toys/E. Rosen Bunny with Easter egg candy container, 1950s, not embossed. Yellow plastic with black paint, 5" x 3.50". *Courtesy of Suzy and Dale Thomas. $25-35.*

Chick with umbrella rattle, 1950s, embossed U.S.A. Pink and white plastic with blue paint, 3" x 2.75". *Author's Collection. $20-35.*

Chick egg cup, 1950s, not embossed, . Made in U.S.A. Red, brown, green, and yellow plastic with green paint, 3.50" x 2.50". *Author's Collection. $35-45.*

Easter basket, 1950s-1960s. Made in U.S.A. Yellow plastic, 8" x 6".
Courtesy of Richard Miller, Photo by Richard Miller. $20-35.

Easter basket with wire bail, 1950s. Made in U.S.A. Green plastic
with yellow paint, 8.50" x 5". *Author's Collection.* $35-50.

E. Rosen Easter sucker holder 1950s not embossed. Green and white
plastic with purple paint. 4" by 1.75" . *Author's Collection.* $15-20

E. Rosen Easter sucker holders, 1950s, not embossed. Yellow and pink
plastic with green paint, 4" x 1.75". *Author's Collection.* $15-20 each.

Irwin pink nesting Bunny, 1950s, embossed, Irwin, U.S.A. Pink plastic, 6" x 4".
Courtesy of Bertram M. Cohen, Irwin Plastics Corporation Estate Collection. $50-65.

Hen with Chicks pull toy, 1950s, not embossed.
Made in U.S.A. Blue, pink, and yellow plastic with
red paint, 7" x 7". *Author's Collection. $45-65.*

Clicker Duck Easter toy, 1950s, not embossed, .
Made in U.S.A. Red and yellow plastic with black
and white paint, the feet act as a trigger for the
mouth to open and close, 4.50" x 2.50". *Author's
Collection. $35-45.*

Mattel Chick pulling wagon candy container, 1940s-1950s, metal and wooden cart.
The chick is yellow plastic with red paint, 9" x 4.50". *Author's Collection. $75-100.*

Commonwealth Magicians Rabbit out of hat party favor, 1940s, embossed, Commonwealth Plastics Corporation. Blue and white plastic, 3" x 3". *Author's Collection. $45-65.*

Commonwealth Magician hat Buster Brown party favor, 1940s, embossed, Commonwealth Plastics Corporation. Black and white plastic, 3" x 3". *Author's Collection. $45-65.*

Easter egg with Bunny inside party favor, 1950s, not embossed. Yellow and pink plastic with blue, black and red paint, 3" x 2.50". *Author's Collection. $25-35.*

E. Rosen Bunny candy container, he is wearing overalls, 1940s-1950s, not embossed. Yellow plastic with blue paint, he was purchased wearing this hat, 4" x 2". *Courtesy of Suzy and Dale Thomas. $25-35.*

Knickerbocker Chick in egg rattle, 1950s. Yellow and white plastic with black and red paint, 3" x 3". *Courtesy of Suzy and Dale Thomas. $25-35.*

Marx Bunny pulling cart, 1950s. Yellow, blue and clear plastic, 7" x 4.75". *Courtesy of Richard Miller. Photo by Richard Miller. $65-85.*

Red Bunny rattle, 1950s, not embossed. Made in U.S.A. Red plastic with white paint, 4" x 2". *Courtesy of Dave and Ginny Wellington. $25-35.*

Box for Marx Bunny pulling cart.

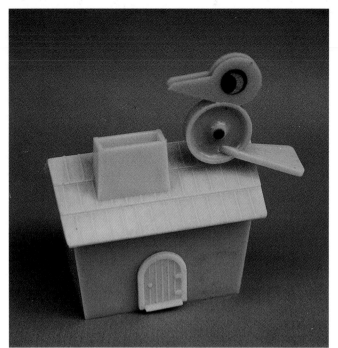

Mattel® Bird house bank, 1950s. Pink and blue plastic with paper eyes, 5"x 5". *Courtesy of Suzy and Dale Thomas. $45-65.*

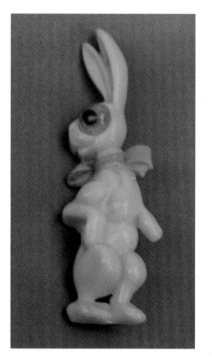

Easter Bunny pin, 1950s, not embossed. Made in U.S.A. Pink plastic with blue paint and googly eyes, 2.50" x 1". *Author's Collection. $18-25.*

Bunny pin, 1950s, not embossed. Made in U.S.A. Blue plastic with black, white, and red paint, 2" x 1". *Author's Collection. $18-25.*

Italian Bunny made of plastic and wood, party favor, 1960s, the head and the baby bunny are wooden and her dress is yellow plastic with red paint, 2.50" x 2". *Author's Collection. $15-20.*

Lamb and Rocking Horse tracers, 1950s, embossed Traceit Toys Pomona Ca. Yellow and green plastic, 10" x 8". *Author's Collection. $10-15 each.*

Chick coming out of egg pop up toy, 1960s, FunWorld, Easter Unlimited. White, yellow and blue plastic, 3" x 2". *Author's Collection.* $18-25.

Easter Baskets holding cupcake sticks, 1950s, not embossed. Made in U.S.A. *Courtesy of Suzy and Dale Thomas. Cupcake sticks, $3-5; baskets, $25-40.*

Knickerbocker boy and girl Bunny banks, 1950s, Leo L. White artist. Pink, brown and yellow plastic with blue, white and red paint, 11" x 4.50". *Author's Collection.* $95-125 each.

Close up of 1950s cupcake sticks. *Author's Collection.* $3-5 each.

170,436
TOY FIGURE
Leo L. White, Beverly Hills, Calif.
Application April 13, 1953, Serial No. 24,477
Term of patent 7 years
(Cl. D34—2)

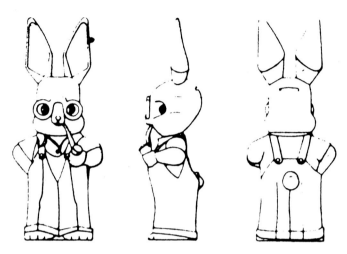

The ornamental design for a toy figure, substantially as shown.

Patent Photo of design patent #170430, Leo L. White artist.

Knickerbocker Bunny with glasses and pipe bank, 1950s, embossed Knickerbocker Plastics Company, North Hollywood, California. Pink and yellow plastic with white and blue paint, 11" x 4.50". *Courtesy of Suzy and Dale Thomas. $95-125.*

158,704
SPECTACLED TOY FIGURE OR THE LIKE
Constance Ray White, Beverly Hills, Calif.
Application November 12, 1949, Serial No. 5,992
Term of patent 14 years
(Cl. D34—4)

The ornamental design for a spectacled toy figure or the like, substantially as shown.

Patent Photo of design patent #158704, Constance Ray White.

Knickerbocker boy and girl bunny rattles, late 1940s-1950s, the girl bunny is embossed Knickerbocker Plastic Company, Glendale, California. Yellow and pink plastic with red, blue and black paint, 4.50" x 2". *Courtesy of Suzy and Dale Thomas. $35-50, each.*

Knickerbocker Praying Bunny rattle, late 1940s, embossed Knickerbocker Plastics Company, Glendale, California. Constance Ray White, artist. Yellow and pink plastic with blue and black paint, 6" x 2.50". *Author's Collection.* $45-65.

Knickerbocker Praying Bunny rattle, late 1940s, embossed Knickerbocker Plastic Company, Glendale, California. Constance Ray White, artist. Pink, yellow and brown plastic with black and blue paint, 6" x 2.50". *Author's Collection.* $45-65.

Knickerbocker Praying Bunny rattle, late 1940s, embossed Knickerbocker Plastics Company, Glendale, California. Constance Ray White, artist. Yellow, brown, and pink plastic with blue and black paint, 6" x 2.50". *Author's Collection.* $45-65.

Knickerbocker Praying Bunny, late 1940s, embossed Knickerbocker Plastic Company, Glendale, California. Constance Ray White artist. Pink and yellow plastic with blue paint, 6" x 2.50". *Author's Collection.* $45-65.

Knickerbocker Boy Bunny rattle, late 1940s, embossed, Knickerbocker Plastics Company, Glendale, California, pat. pend. Constance Ray White, artist. Yellow plastic with blue and black paint, 4.50" x 1.50". *Courtesy of Suzy and Dale Thomas. $30-45.*

Knickerbocker Boy and Girl rattle, late 1940s, embossed Knickerbocker Plastics Company, Glendale, California, pat. pend. Constance Ray White, artist. Pink plastic with blue and black paint, 4.50" x 1.50". *Author's Collection. $30-45 each.*

Knickerbocker Bunny with carrot, 1950s, embossed Knickerbocker Plastics Company design pat. pend. Artist unknown. Red and yellow plastic with brown and black paint, the carrot pulls away from his mouth as his ears move, 4.50" x 4". *Author's Collection. $35-45.*

Knickerbocker unmarked Bunny rattles, late 1940s-1950s. Pink and yellow plastic with blue and green paint, 4" x 2". *Courtesy of Suzy and Dale Thomas. $20-30 each.*

Knickerbocker bunny on wheels, late 1940s-1950s, embossed, Knickerbocker plastics Co. Glendale Cal. Yellow and red plastic with blue and red paint, cart is missing, 4" by 3.5". *Courtesy of Mark and Judy Craven. Photo by Mark Craven. $35-50.*

Knickerbocker Bunny pulling cart on wheels, candy container, late 1940s-1950s, embossed Knickerbocker Plastics Company, Glendale, California. The bunny in the cart appears to be the art work of Constance Ray White, it is not embossed. Blue and pink plastic with red, white and black paint, bunny with cart is 7" x 4". *Author's Collection. $95-125, for bunny with cart.*

A close up of Bunny in cart appears to be part of a Knickerbocker toy. *Author's Collection. $25-35.*

Knickerbocker running Bunny rattle, late 1940s, not embossed. Yellow plastic with blue and red paint, 3.75" x 3.75". *Author's Collection. $25-40.*

Knickerbocker Bunny with cart, 1950s, embossed Knickerbocker North Hollywood, California. Pink plastic with blue and orange paint, 4.50" x 3". *Author's Collection.* $40-55.

Knickerbocker Chick with cart, candy container, 1950s, embossed Knickerbocker North Hollywood, California. Yellow plastic with orange and blue paint, 4.50" x 3". *Author's Collection.* $40-55.

Knickerbocker Bunny with cart, candy container, 1950s, embossed Knickerbocker North Hollywood, California. Yellow plastic with orange and blue paint, 4.50" x 3". *Author's Collection.* $40-55.

Knickerbocker Sitting Bunny rattles, late 1940s-1950s, embossed Knickerbocker Plastic Company Glendale, California. Yellow plastic with blue and red paint, 3" x 2". *Author's Collection.* $25-35 each.

Knickerbocker Rocking Lamb rattle, late 1940s-1950s, embossed Knickerbocker Plastic Company Glendale, California, design pat. pend. Blue plastic with pink paint, 4" x 2.50". *Courtesy of Suzy and Dale Thomas.* $35-50.

Knickerbocker Rocking Lamb rattle, late 1940s-1950s, embossed Knickerbocker Plastic Company Glendale, California, design pat. pend. Pink plastic with blue paint, 4" x 2.50". *Author's Collection* $35-50.

Knickerbocker Rocking Elephant rattle, late 1940s-1950s, embossed Knickerbocker Plastic Company Glendale, California, design pat. pend. Pink plastic with blue, red, and black paint, 4" x 3". *Author's Collection* $35-50.

Knickerbocker Pig rattle, late 1940s-1950s, embossed, Knickerbocker Plastic Company Glendale, California, design pat. pend. Pink plastic with black and red paint, 4" x 2.50". *Author's Collection.* $35-55.

Knickerbocker Hen and Rooster with Chicks Easter toys, late 1940s-1950s. Rooster and Hen are embossed Knickerbocker. Chicks are embossed with design pat. #150163. This patent number was assigned to a entirely different object unrelated to Knickerbocker. Red, yellow, and white plastic with orange and red paint, Hen is 3" x 2.50", Rooster is 4" x 3.50", small Chicks are 2" x 1". *Author's Collection.* $95-125.

Knickerbocker Rooster rattles, late 1940s-1950s, embossed Knickerbocker, Glendale, California. Pink and yellow plastic with red, brown, green, and blue paint, 4" x 3.50". *Courtesy of Suzy and Dale Thomas.* $20-35 each.

Knickerbocker Hen rattle, embossed Knickerbocker. Yellow plastic with brown, orange, black and green paint, 3" x 2.50". *Courtesy of Suzy and Dale Thomas.* $25-35 each.

Knickerbocker Chick rattles, late 1940s-1950s, embossed Kinckerbocker Plastic Company Glendale, California. Yellow plastic with orange and black paint, 3.50" x 2". *Author's Collection. $25-35.*

Knickerbocker Duck vase, 1950s, embossed Knickerbocker patent pending. Green and yellow plastic with orange, black, and white paint, 5" x 3". *Courtesy of Suzy and Dale Thomas. $35-50.*

Knickerbocker Skipper the Duck #350 baby rattle, late 1940s-1950s, embossed Knickerbocker Plastics patent pending. Pink plastic with orange, black and white paint, original box, 2.50" x 3". *Author's Collection. $35-50.*

Knickerbocker Chick vase, 1950s, embossed Knickerbocker Plastics Company Glendale, California. Blue and pink plastic with orange and black paint, 5" x 4". *Courtesy of Suzy and Dale Thomas. $35-50.*

Collection of Knickerbocker bathtub and Easter toys. *Author's Collection.*

Knickerbocker hen with eggs large bank, 1950s, embossed Knickerbocker Glendale, California. Pink plastic with blue, orange and white paint, 9" x 6". *Courtesy of Suzy and Dale Thomas.* $75-95.

Knickerbocker Chick rattle, late 1940s-1950s, embossed Knickerbocker Plastic Company Glendale, California, some of these chicks are embossed, patent pend. Blue plastic with orange paint, 4.50" x 2.50". *Author's Collection.* $30-45.

164,463
TOY FIGURINE OR SIMILAR ARTICLE
Constance Ray White, Beverly Hills, Calif.
Application November 9, 1950, Serial No. 12,920
Term of patent 7 years
(Cl. D34—2)

The ornamental design for a toy figurine or similar article, substantially as shown.

Knickerbocker Pig with glasses bank, 1940s-1950s, embossed Knickerbocker Plastic Company Glendale, California. Constance Ray White, artist. Green and yellow plastic with brown, pink, and black paint, 5" x 3". *Author's Collection.* $45-65.

Patent photo for design patent #164463, Constance Ray White, artist.

 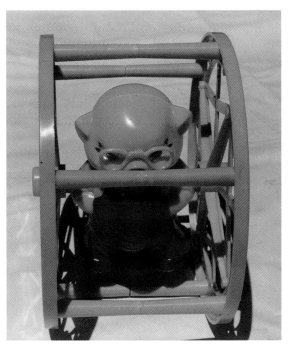 

Knickerbocker Pig bank, made without glasses and metal bank plug, late 1940s-1950s, embossed Knickerbocker Plastic Company, Glendale, California. Constance Ray White, artist. Yellow plastic with pink, black, and red paint, 8" x 5". *Author's Collection. $85-125.*

Knickerbocker Pig with glasses roly poly toy, 1950s, embossed Knickerbocker Plastic Company, Glendale, California. Pink and yellow plastic with red and black paint, 9" in diameter. *Author's Collection. $85-100.*

Irwin Plastics Corporation Estate Collection Pig, 1930s-1940s nonflammable celluloid. *Courtesy of Bertram M. Cohen. $65-95.*

Twin Knickerbocker Pig banks, late 1940s-1950s, embossed Knickerbocker Plastic Company, Glendale, California. Constance Ray White, artist. Pink plastic with black, pink and blue paint, 4.50" x 3". *Author's Collection. $30-45.*

Pig bank, 1950s-1960s not embossed. Made in U.S.A. Green plastic with black writing, 4.50" x 3". *Author's Collection. $25-30.*

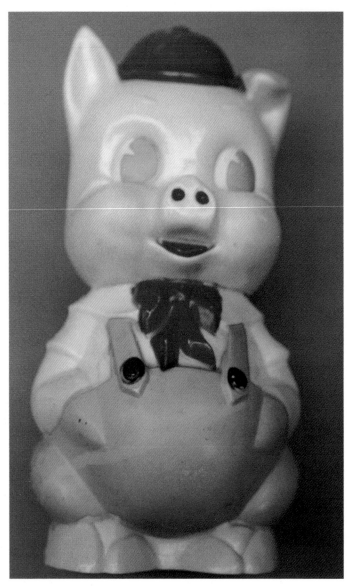

Ideal Pig bank, 1950s. Pink plastic with blue, yellow, red and black paint, 12" x 6.50". *Author's Collection. $75-100.*

Owl and Pig banks, 1950s-1960s, Owl is embossed. Made in U.S.A. Pig is not embossed. Pink and blue plastic, L. 4" x 2", R. 3.50" x 2.75". *Author's Collection. $20-30, each.*

Red Goose and Pig banks, 1940s-1950s, not embossed. Made in U.S.A. Red and pink plastic, L. 4.50" x 2.50", R. 3.50" x 2.75". *Author's Collection. $25-30, each.*

Pig banks, 1950s-1960s, not embossed. Made in U.S.A. Red and green plastic with red paint, L. 3.50" x 2.75", R. 4" x 2.50". *Author's Collection. $20-30 each.*

Pig bank, 1950s-1960s, West Land Plastic Newberry Park, California. Pink plastic with yellow hat that tips when you put money in the bank. The Pig on the right is missing his hat, 4.25" x 7". *Author's Collection. $15-25.*

Pig bank, 1960s, not embossed. Made in U.S.A. Pink plastic, 7.50" x 5.50". *Author's Collection. $15-25.*

Above: Aladdin Pig baby rattle, 1950s, embossed Aladdin U.S.A. Blue plastic with yellow, white and red paint, 4" x 3". *Courtesy of Suzy and Dale Thomas. $25-40.*

Left: Pig banks, 1940s-1950s, not embossed. Made in U.S.A. Pink and yellow plastic, 4.50" x 3". *Author's Collection. $20-30 each.*

Aladdin Elephant baby room plate, 1950s, embossed Aladdin U.S.A. Pink and blue plastic with red, white and black paint, 6" in diameter. *Author's Collection. $25-40.*

Aladdin Mouse baby rattle, 1950s, embossed Aladdin U.S.A. Pink plastic with black, blue and white paint, 4" x 2". *Author's Collection. $25-40.*

E. Rosen vinyl Bunny on wheel, 1960s, not embossed. Green and yellow plastic, yellow vinyl with green paint, 7" x 3.50". *Courtesy of Suzy and Dale Thomas. $15-25.*

Hard plastic candy stick Bunny head, 1950s-1960s, not embossed. Made in U.S.A. Pink plastic with purple paint, 8" x 3.50". *Courtesy of Suzy and Dale Thomas. $15-25.*

Vinyl, made in Japan, 1960s Chick, embossed, Japan. Peach vinyl with blue, yellow, red, black, and white paint, 6" x 4". *Author's Collection. $15-25.*

Tomy mother Rabbit with baby walker, 1970s, embossed Tomy, made in Japan. Flesh color, white, gray, green plastic with white, blue, pink, yellow, and black paint. The little Bunny comes out of the carriage and is a walker too, 4.50" x 4". *Author's Collection.* $20-35.

Bunny candy containers from West Germany, heads are made of vinyl, 1960s. Yellow, blue, green, and red plastic with white, red, and blue paint, 7.50" x 3.50". *Author's Collection.* $15-25 each.

Fun World Bunny and Ducks on rollers, early 1960s, made in Hong Kong. White plastic with blue, orange, yellow, green, pink, dark blue, and black paint, 5" x 2.50". *Author's Collection.* $20-35 each.

Fun World Bunny on spring, 1990s, made in China, embossed China. Green and yellow plastic with yellow, black, and red paint, 4.50" x 2". *Author's Collection.* $5-8.

Fun World bunny in car, early 1960s, made in Hong Kong. White plastic with yellow, green, pink and silver paint. 3" x 3", bottom part is missing. *Private Collection.* $10-15.

E. Rosen Treasure Hunt Egg, 1950s-1960s. Blue, green, and clear plastic, 3" x 1.75". *Author's Collection.* $15-18 each.

VALENTINE'S, HALLOWEEN, AND THANKSGIVING

E. Rosen Valentine characters candy containers, late 1940s-1950s, not embossed. Hard plastic wedding ring box by Cousins, Valentine box from the 1940s. White plastic with red paint, 3.50" x 2". *Author's Collection.* $35-45 each, box $45.

E. Rosen boxed Valentine character candy containers, late 1940s-1950s, not embossed. White and red plastic with white and red paint, box is 10" x 4". *Courtesy of Suzy and Dale Thomas.* $175-225.

E. Rosen springy head Valentine character candy container, late 1940s-1950s not embossed. White plastic with red paint. 6" x 3". *Courtesy of Mark and Judy Craven, Photo By Mark Craven. $95-125.*

E. Rosen Springy Head Valentine character, candy containers, late 1940s-1950s, not embossed. White plastic with red paint, 6" x 3". *Courtesy of Richard Miller, Photo by Richard Miller. $95-125 each.*

E. Rosen western horse candy container on wheels, late 1940s-1950s, not embossed. White and red plastic, 4.5" x 5". *Courtesy of Mark and Judy Craven, Photo by Mark Craven. $135-150.*

E. Rosen springy head Valentine character candy container, late 1940s-1950s, not embossed. White plastic with red and black paint, 6" x 3" *Courtesy of Mark and Judy Craven, Photo by Mark Craven. $95-125.*

E. Rosen Valentine character, candy containers, late 1940s-1950s, not embossed. White and red plastic with blue, red and flesh paint, 4.50" x 3". *Courtesy of Richard Miller, Photo by Richard Miller. $75-95 each.*

E. Rosen Valentine Cowboy, candy container on wheels, late 1940s-1950s, not embossed. Yellow, green and white plastic with blue, red and flesh paint, 4" x 3". *Courtesy of Richard Miller, Photo by Richard Miller. $65-85.*

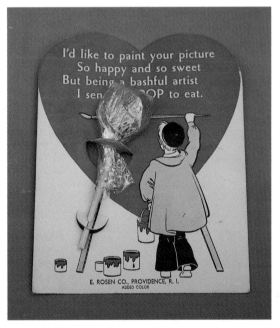

E. Rosen paper Valentine, 1950s. The card is 6" x 5". *Author's Collection. $20-35.*

E. Rosen Valentine character, candy containers, late 1940s - 1950's, the clown is embossed Rosbro Plastics. White, red and yellow plastic with blue, red and flesh paint, cowgirl is 4.50" x 3", clown is 5" x 3". *Author's Collection. $75-95 each.*

E. Rosen Valentine Cowboy and Heart candy containers, late 1940s-1950s, not embossed. Red and white plastic with black, red and flesh paint, hearts are 2.50" x 2", cowboy is 3" x 3". *Author's Collection. Hearts $25-35 each, cowboy $35-55.*

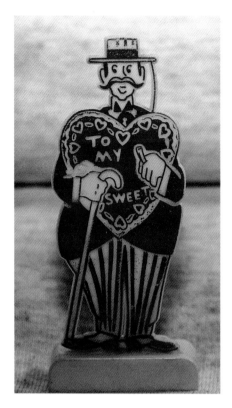

E. Rosen Gay 90s Valentine sucker holder, 1950s, not embossed. White plastic with red paint. 3.5" tall. *Courtesy of Mark and Judy Craven, Photo by Mark Craven. $25-35.*

E. Rosen Cowboy with Western horse pulling Valentine wagon, candy container, late 1940s-1950s. White plastic with red, black and flesh paint, 5.50" x 8". *Courtesy of Mark and Judy Craven $300-375.*

E. Rosen Valentine character sucker holder, Humpty Dumpty, late 1940s-1950s, not embossed. 5" x 2.50". *Author's Collection. $20-35.*

E. Rosen Valentine car, candy container, late 1940s-1950s, car is embossed Rosbro Plastics. Red, white, yellow and black plastic, 6.5" x 6.5". *Courtesy of Richard Miller. Photo by Richard Miller. $195-225.*

E. Rosen Valentine car, candy container, late 1940s-1950s, car is embossed Rosbro Plastics. Red, white, yellow, black and pink plastic, 6.50" x 6.50". *Courtesy of Suzy and Dale Thomas.* $195-225.

E. Rosen Valentine car, candy container, late 1940s-1950s. Car is embossed "Rosbro Plastic". Red, white, black, pink, and yellow plastic with blue, red, black and flesh paint, 6.6" x 6.5". *Courtesy of Mark and Judy Craven. Photo by Mark Craven.* $195-225.

E. Rosen Valentine Cowboy, candy containers, late 1940s-1950s, not embossed. Yellow and white plastic with red, black, and flesh paint, 3" x 3". *Courtesy of Suzy and Dale Thomas.* $35-55.

E. Rosen/Tico Toys Valentine Dalmation, candy container on wheels, late 1940s-1950s, not embossed. Red and white plastic with black and red paint, 3.50" x 5", rare. *Courtesy of Suzy and Dale Thomas.* $125-150.

E. Rosen/Tico Toys Valentine whistles, late 1940s-1950s, not embossed. White plastic with red paint, 3" x 1.50". *Courtesy of Suzy and Dale Thomas. $30-45 each.*

E. Rosen Valentine Girl Car candy container, late1940s-1950s, not embossed. Red, white, and green plastic with red, blue, and flesh paint, 4.25" x 2.5". *Courtesy of Mark and Judy Craven. Photo by Mark Craven. $150-200.*

E. Rosen Valentine or Christmas Donkey, candy container, late 1940s-1950s, not embossed. White and green plastic with red paint, 5.5" x 5". *Courtesy of Mark and Judy Craven. Photo by Mark Craven. $135-165*

E. Rosen Valentine boy Car candy container, late 1940s-1950s, not embossed. Red, yellow, and white plastic with blue, flesh and red paint. 4.25" x 5". *Courtesy of Mark and Judy Craven. Photo by Mark Craven. $150-200.*

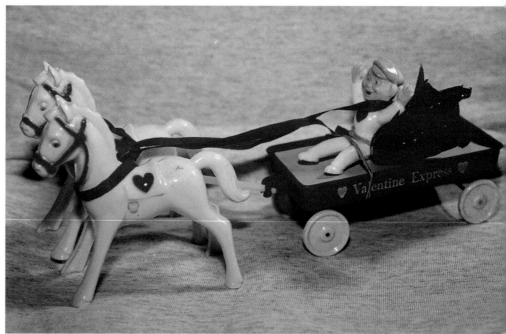

E. Rosen Valentine Express candy container late 1940s-1950s, not embossed. White, red, and yellow plastic with red, blue, and flesh paint, 10" x 5.5". *Courtesy of Mark and Judy Craven. Photo by Mark Craven.* $195-225.

Hard plastic Valentine Heart box, 1940s. Made in U.S.A. Clear plastic, 10" x 10". *Author's Collection.* $10-25.

Hard plastic Valentine dolls. The doll on the left is a Marcie doll. The doll on the right is a Dutchess doll, late 1940s-1950s, 7.50". *Author's Collection.* $24-45 each.

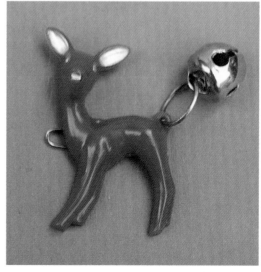

Valentine Deer pin, 1950s. Made in U.S.A. This pin was made for all holidays. Red plastic with white paint, 2" x 1.50". *Author's Collection.* $15-25.

Sweetheart moneybox, 1940s. Yellow clear plastic, 3" x 3".
Author's Collection. $20-35.

Union Products Witch #305, early 1950s. Orange plastic with black paint, 5.25" x 5". *Author's Collection. $250-300.*

E. Rosen Witch with JOL, candy container, early 1950s, embossed Rosbro Plastics. Orange plastic with black, white, red, and flesh paint. *Author's Collection. $35-55.*

E. Rosen Witch on Motorcycle, early 1950s. Orange and green plastic with black paint, 4.88" x 6.88". *Author's Collection. $350-400.*

E. Rosen JOL with Witch and Cat sucker holder, 1950s, not embossed, 2.88" x 3.88". Original price tag $.10. *Courtesy of Mark and Judy Craven. $45-60.*

E. Rosen Cat holding JOL candy container, 1950s, not embossed. Orange plastic with black paint, 5" x 3.50". *Courtesy of Mark and Judy Craven. $65-85.*

Witch head wind up toy, Hallmark® Cards Inc. Made in China, 1990s. Painted green, orange, black and purple, the eyes go back and forth, 2" x 2". *Author's Collection. $15-20.*

Above: Knickerbocker Halloween Elephant rattle, 1950s, embossed Knickerbocker Plastic Company, Glendale, California. Original black and orange paint over white plastic, 4" x 3", very rare. *Author's Collection. $45-65.*

Right: Halloween sucker holders, late 1940s-1950s, not embossed. The one on the left is made in U.S.A., the one on the right is E. Rosen. Green, white, and orange plastic with black and orange paint, L. 3.50" x 1.50, R. 4.38" x 2.50. *Author's Collection. L. $25-35 each, R. $35-45.*

E. Rosen/Tico Toy Cat pushing JOL, candy container, late 1940s-1950s, not embossed. Orange and yellow plastic with green and black paint, 5.25" x 6.75". *Author's Collection.* *$250-275.*

E. Rosen/Tico Toy Halloween whistle, late 1940s-1950s, not embossed. Yellow plastic with black paint, 3" x 2.50". *Author's Collection.* *$35-50.*

Union Products #99JOL and #98Candy Jack, 1950s. Orange plastic with green, black and white paint, L. 5.25" x 6", R. 3.50" x 5". *Author's Collection. L. $45-65, R. $25-45.*

E. Rosen/Tico Toys JOL's candy containers, 1940s-1950s, not embossed. Orange plastic with white and black paint, L. 3.50" x 4.50", R. 4" x 4.88". *Author's Collection. L. $45-65, R. $35-45 top missing.*

String of hard plastic Halloween lights, 1950s. Orange plastic with black paint. Made in U.S.A. *Courtesy of Mark and Judy Craven. Photo by Mark Craven. $125-150.*

Plastic Turkey cupcake stick, 1960s. Made in Hong Kong. Painted black, white, red, gold, green, and yellow, 2.50" x 1". *Author's Collection. $5-8.*

Plastic Turkey, candy container, 1960s. Made in Hong Kong. Painted black, white, red, gold, green, and yellow, 3" x 3". *Author's Collection. $20-35.*

E. Rosen Turkey candy container, not embossed. White plastic with brown, red, and orange paint, 3.50" x 3.50". *Courtesy of Dave and Ginny Wellington. $35-50.*

118

Photo of Witch Collection. *Private Collection of The Witch Lady of L.A.*

OTHER OCCASIONS

Party candy and nut cups, 1950s, embossed Best U.S.A. White, pink, blue, and yellow plastic, 3" in diameter. *Author's Collection. $5-8 each.*

Above: Party candy and nut cups, 1950s, embossed Gilbert Plastics, Hillside, New Jersey. Pink and white plastic with a nametag, 3" in diameter. *Author's Collection. $8-12 each.*

Left: Party candy and nut cups, 1950s, the clover nut cup in the front is embossed B with and upside down A. The other three cups are embossed Gilbert Plastics, Hillside, New Jersey. Yellow and white plastic, 3" in diameter. *Author's Collection. $8-12 each.*

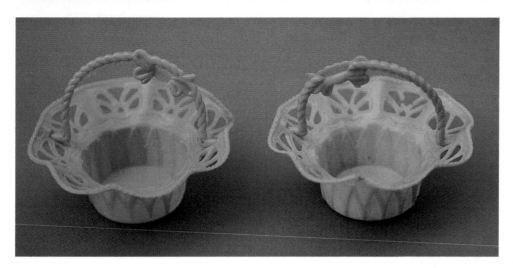

Party candy and nut cups, 1950s, not embossed. Made in U.S.A. Pink an blue plastic, 3" in diameter. *Author's Collection. $5-8 each.*

Circus theme party candy and nut cup, 1950s, embossed Best U.S.A. Red plastic, 3" x 2". *Author's Collection. $8-12.*

Valentine party candy and nut cup, 1950s, embossed Best U.S.A. Made in U.S.A. Red and white plastic, 3" x 2.50". *Author's Collection. $18-22.*

Party candy and nut cup with ribbon on handle, 1950s, embossed Best U.S.A. White plastic, 3" x 3". *Courtesy of Suzy and Dale Thomas. $5-8.*

Christmas party candy and nut cups, 1950s, the red cup has a bow handle and is embossed Best U.S.A. The green cups were made without handles and are not embossed. Made in U.S.A. Green and red plastic, 3" in diameter. *Author's Collection. $5-8.*

Birthday cake plastic flowers, 1950s. Made in U.S.A. Painted pink, blue, and green plastic, 1" x 1". *Author's Collection. $1-2, each.*

Swan candy and nut cup with ballerina cake decorations,1960s, not embossed. Pink plastic swan with pink vinyl ballerinas with silver, gold, red and black paint, swan is 4" x 2.50", Ballerinas are 2.50" tall. *Author's Collection. $3-5 each.*

Umbrella party favors with Irwin novelty Kewpie, the umbrellas are embossed Best U.S.A. Pink and white plastic, the doll is embossed Irwin Plastics, umbrellas are 3" in diameter, the doll is 4" tall. *Author's Collection. Umbrellas $10-18 each, dolls $20-35.*

121

Birthday candleholders, 1940s. Made in U.S.A. Blue plastic on original card, card is 4" x 3.75". *Author's Collection. $15-25.*

Birthday candleholders, 1940s. Made in U.S.A. Cowboy and Indian theme, blue plastic, 2" x 1.50". *Courtesy of Tom and Terry Weber. $15-20.*

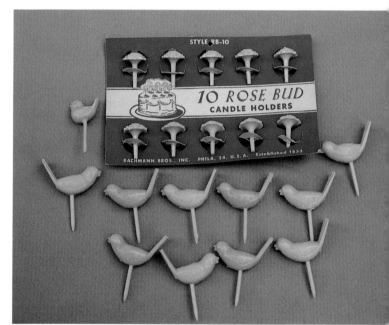

Bird and Rose bud candle holders, 1960s-1950s. Made in U.S.A. The rose bud candleholders are from Bachmann Brothers Inc., established in 1833. Pink and blue plastic, birds are 1.50" x 1.50", rose buds are 1". *Author's Collection. $10-15 each set.*

Birthday candleholders, circus theme, 1950s. Made in U.S.A. Pink and blue plastic, 1.50" x 1.50". *Author's Collection. $18-20 a set.*

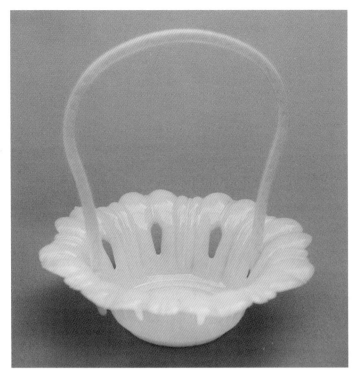

Party candy and nut cup, 1950s, embossed A Carnival Production. Made in U.S.A. Yellow plastic, 5" x 5". *Author's Collection.* $20-25.

Mickey Mouse® candy and nut cup, 1950s, embossed Walt Disney Productions. Made in U.S.A. Pink plastic, 2.50" x 3.50". These cups also came as many other Disney® characters. *Author's Collection.* $25-35.

Indian and Elephant party horns, 1950s. Made in U.S.A. Yellow, green, and pink plastic with blue paint and red vinyl ears and feathers, 6.50" x 3". *Courtesy of Suzy and Dale Thomas.* $18-25 each.

Paper and plastic party horns, 1950s. Made in U.S.A. Yellow, white, and red plastic heads with red and white paint, 6.50" x 2.50". *Author's Collection.* $18-25 each.

Party favor Circus train, late 1940s-1950s, embossed Banner U.S.A. Yellow, blue, pink, and red cars, there were also other colors of train cars that are not shown. *Author's Collection.* $5-8 each.

Blondie's cookie cutter, party favor, Copyright©1956, King Features Syndicate Inc., on original card. *Courtesy of Suzy and Dale Thomas. $35-50.*

Girls party favor doll clothes hanger, 1950s, embossed Totsy, Springfield, Massachusetts. Pink plastic, 6" x 2.50". *Author's Collection. $4-8.*

Cameo children's party play dishes, 1950s. Made in U.S.A. Blue and white plastic, this is not a complete set. *Author's Collection. $25.*

Knickerbocker Puss and Boots jack in the box. Red and yellow plastic with red, white, and black paint, 5" x 7.50" open. *Childhood toy of Suzy Thomas. $40-65.*

Girl scout pin, 1950s. Made in U.S.A. Flesh plastic with brown, red and yellow paint, 2.75" x 1.75". *Author's Collection. $25-35.*

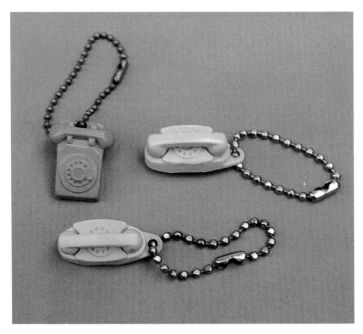

Rotary dial collectible telephone key chain party favors, 1950s-1960s. Made in U.S.A. Tan, pink, and blue plastic, the pink and blue phones are Princess Telephones. These were given away free by the Phone Company. *Author's Collection. $3-5 each.*

Bubble gum machine charms or party favors, 1940s-1950s. Made in U.S.A. Red, tan, green, and blue plastic, the small charm has a 1940s style metallic over plastic coat. *Author's Collection. $3-5 each.*

First day of Spring pin, robin going after worm. Made in U.S.A. Painted green, brown, red, and yellow and white plastic, 2.50" x 1.75". *Author's Collection. $20-30.*

Irwin Plastics miniature tea set, party favor, 1950s. All clear plastic, childhood toy of Sandra Weis. *Author's Collection. $25-40 complete.*

Dutchess doll for the Fourth of July, embossed Dutchess Doll Corporation, Dolls of All Nations 1948, 7.50". *Author's Collection. $35-45.*

Dutchess doll for Saint Patrick's Day, embossed Dutchess Doll Corporation 1948, 7.50". Boxed for Continental Dolls. The Dutchess Doll Corporation dressed Dolls for All Nations and also sold their dolls to other companies to be dressed and boxed with different company names. *Author's Collection. $35-4.*

Irwin celluloid novelty doll, 1930s. *Courtesy of Bertram M. Cohen, Irwin Plastics Corporation Estate Collection. $100-125.*

Irwin celluloid novelty doll, 1930s. *Courtesy of Bertram M. Cohen, Irwin Plastics Corporation Estate Collection. $100-125.*

Irwin celluloid novelty doll boy with bunny rattle. *Courtesy of Bertram M. Cohen, Irwin Plastics Corporation Estate Collection. $100-125.*

Irwin celluloid mechanical doll mobile novelty toy with box. *Courtesy of Bertram M. Cohen, Irwin Plastics Corporation Estate Collection. $75-95.*

Irwin hard plastic Flamenco dancer mechanical wind up toy, 1950s, 6.25" tall. *Courtesy of Bertram M. Cohen, Irwin Plastics Corporation Estate Collection. $150-175.*

Irwin hard plastic Georgie the Whistling Boy named after Irwin Cohn's son. In 1951 Irwin Toys introduced the first plastic mechanical toys to America. They were wound by a metal key and were an instant success. Georgie and Nina, Mother's helper, were among the first mechanical toys. Nina was Irwin Cohn's daughter (no picture). Georgie is 9.75" tall, air flowed through two small holes in his belt buckle to make the whistle. Italian artist Perugi designed many of the Irwin toys. *Courtesy of Bertram M. Cohen, Irwin Plastics Corporation Estate Collection. $200-250 in box.*

Irwin hard plastic novelty dolls, 1950s, party favors. Green and yellow plastic with flesh and black paint, 3.75" tall. *Courtesy of Bertram M. Cohen, Irwin Plastics Corporation Estate Collection. $25-40 each.*

Irwin celluloid doll rattle, 1930s. 3.75" tall. *Courtesy of Bertram M. Cohen, Irwin Plastics Corporation Estate Collection.* $65-85.

Irwin celluloid Pink Riding Hood, 1930s. *Courtesy of Bertram M. Cohen, Irwin Plastics Corporation Estate Collection.* $55-65.

Irwin celluloid baby doll in robe rattle. *Courtesy of Bertram M. Cohen, Irwin Plastics Corporation Estate Collection.* $55-65.

Dime Store party favor perfume bottles, 1950s. Made in U.S.A., 4" x 1.50". *Author's Collection.* $20-25 each.

German plastic pencil sharpener, party favor, 1950s, rare, 2.50" x 2.50", with horsehair tail. Childhood toy of Charles Shock, Jr. *Author's Collection.* $30-45.

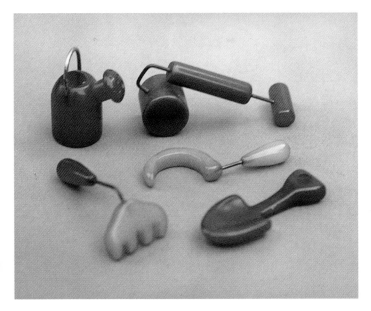

Bakelite party favors in miniature, 1930s, childhood toys of Auntie Lucille Wunsch. *Author's Collection. $125.*

Jiminy Cricket drinking cup with flashing googly eyes, 1950s. Made in U.S.A., 4" x 3". *Courtesy of Suzy and Dale Thomas. $35-55.*

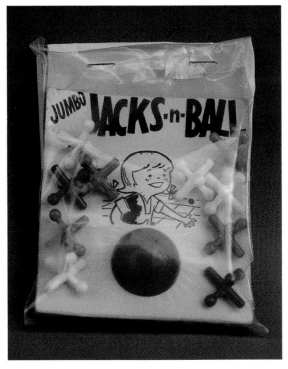

Jacks and ball party favor, 1950s. Made in U.S.A. Card is 4" x 3.50". *Courtesy of Suzy and Dale Thomas. $15-25.*

Jacks and ball Little Miss party favor, 1950s. Made in U.S.A. With vinyl purse, 6" x 4". *Author's Collection. $20-35.*

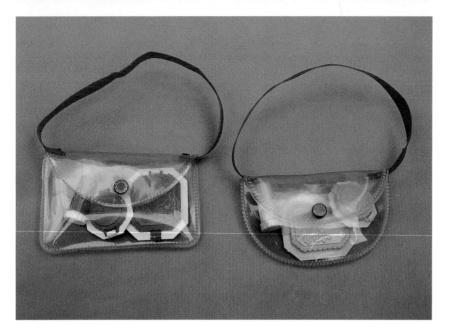

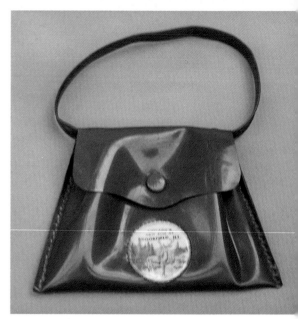

Party favor make up kits with vinyl purses, 1950s. Made in U.S.A. 6" x 4". *Author's Collection.* $20-35 each.

Souvenir purse in vinyl from the Brookfield Zoo, Chicago, Illinois. 6" x 5". *Author's Collection.* $25-35.

Wheelbarrows with tools, party favors, 1950s, Commonwealth Plastics. Red, yellow, blue, and pink plastic with matching colored tools, 3.50" x 1.50". *Author's Collection.* $25-35 complete set.

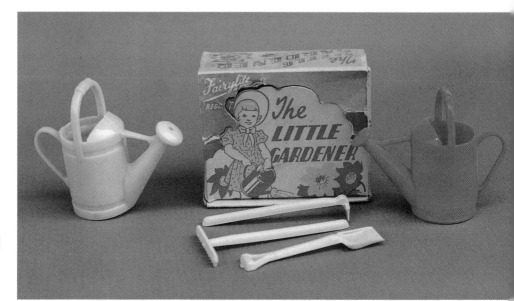

Fairylite little gardener watering can and tools party favor, 1950s. Made in England. *Courtesy of Suzy and Dale Thomas.* $25-35.

Babys in plastic sleigh pulled by dachshund party favor, Acme Toy Company, late 1940s-1950s, the babies and the dog are old vinyl and should not be stored together with the plastic sleigh because the old vinyl decomposes and melts into the plastic, 4.5" x 1.5". *Author's Collection. $25-40.*

Irwin celluloid dog rattle, 1930s. *Courtesy of Bertram M. Cohen, Irwin Plastics CorporationEstate Collection. $65-85.*

Ideal doghouse with rubber dog, party favor, 1950s, embossed Ideal. Red and white plastic with brown rubber dog, 2.50" x 2.50". *Courtesy of Suzy and Dale Thomas. $25-35.*

Above: Ideal doll house television,1950s. Brown plastic with colored pictures that change when you turn the handle, 4" x 3.50". *Author's Collection. $45-65.*

Left: Emerson Ultra-wave Television novelty bank, late 1940s-1950s, give away. Brown plastic with original clown picture, 4" x 2.50". *Author's Collection. $45-65.*

Renwal rocket car and truck, party favors, 1940s-1950s, embossed A Renwal Product. Blue, pink, and yellow plastic, L. 4.25" x 2.50", R 4.25" x 1.50". *Author's Collection. $25-45 each.*

Ideal dollhouse hutch,1950s. Brown plastic with top that opens, 7.50" x 4". Childhood toy of Susan Schmitz. *Author's Collection. $55-75.*

General Douglas Mac Arthur hard plastic,1940s pin. Painted brown shades with flesh color, 2.50" x 2". *Author's Collection. $35-45.*

Bowling party novelty favor place card holder,1960s. Made in Hong Kong. Yellow and black plastic with brown, tan, red, and black paint, box is 4" x 3". *Author's Collection. $25-40.*

Renwal and Marx car, party favors, 1940s-1950s. Red plastic with plastic and rubber tires, Renwal L. 4" x 1.75", Marx R. 6" x 2.50". *Author's Collection.* $25-45 each.

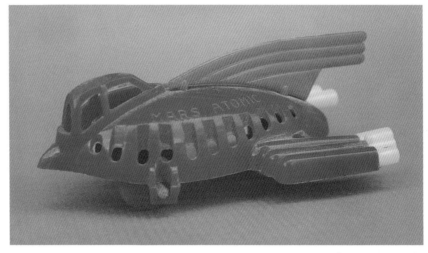

Atomic car party favor, 1950s, embossed Mars Atomic. Made in U.S.A. Blue, red, and yellow plastic, 3.50" x 2". *Courtesy of Suzy and Dale Thomas.* $25-45.

Toy car Collection of Suzy and Dale Thomas.

Cat with bird cage whistle, party favor, early 1960s, embossed Western Germany. Red, yellow, and blue plastic, the bird is on a spring that goes up and down when you whistle, 6" x 2.50". *Author's Collection. $20-35.*

Man riding unicycle, party favor whistle, late 1940s, Commonwealth Plastics Corporation. Red and clear plastic with blue plastic balls that roll around inside when you whistle, 4.50" x 4.50". *Author's Collection. $20-35.*

Clown whistle party favor, 1950s, not embossed. Made in U.S.A. Yellow and green plastic, 4.50" x 1.50". *Courtesy of Suzy and Dale Thomas. $20-35.*

Clown whistle party favor, 1950s, not embossed. Made in U.S.A. White and red plastic, 4.50" x 1.50". *Courtesy of Suzy and Dale Thomas. $20-35.*

Pipe whistle, party favor, 1960s, embossed Western Germany. Brown and yellow plastic, 5.50" x 2". *Author's Collection. $15-20*

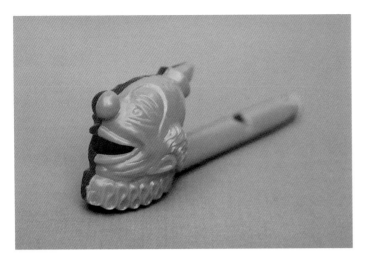

Clown whistle party favor, 1950s, not embossed. Made in U.S.A. Green and red plastic, 4.50" x 1.50". *Courtesy of Suzy and Dale Thomas. $20-35.*

Kiddie pipe party favor on original card, 1950s. Made in U.S.A. Card is 4" x 2". *Courtesy of Suzy and Dale Thomas. $18-25.*

Lional train whistles, party favors, 1950s, embossed Lional. Blue and green plastic, 2.50" x 4". *Courtesy of Suzy and Dale Thomas. $20-35 each.*

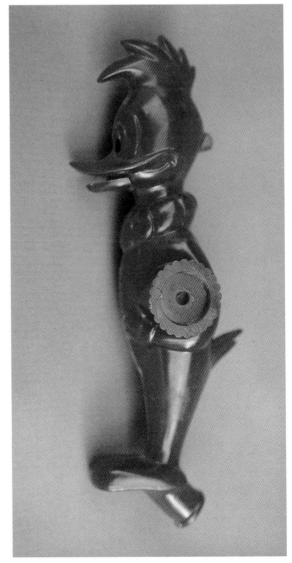

Elmar train whistle, party favor, 1950s. Red plastic, 4" x 3". *Courtesy of Suzy and Dale Thomas. $25-40.*

Woody Woodpecker whistle, party favor, 1950s. Made in U.S.A. Red plastic with black paint, 7" x 2". *Courtesy of Suzy and Dale Thomas. $25-45.*

Gun party favor, 1950s, embossed. Made in U.S.A. Red plastic clicker gun, 5" x 3". *Courtesy of Suzy and Dale Thomas.* $20-35.

E. Rosen candy container gun, 1950s. with original tag. Clear plastic, 5" x 3". *Courtesy of Suzy and Dale Thomas.* $25-40.

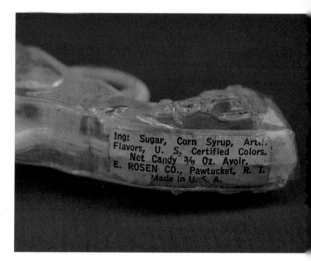

Photo of E. Rosen tag on candy container gun.

Knickerbocker squirt gun, party favor, 1950s, embossed, Knickerbocker, Glendale, California. Black plastic with red rubber plug, 4" x 2.50". *Author's Collection.* $18-25.

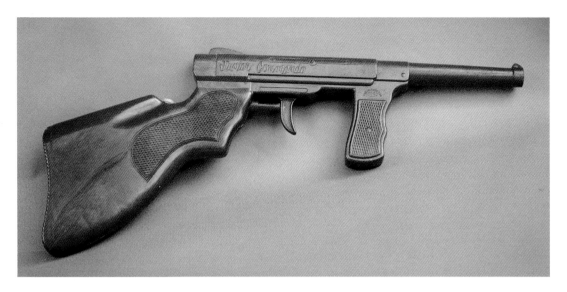

Jr. Commando Tomy Gun, 1950s. Made in U.S.A. Brown and flash plastic, 15" x 7". *Courtesy of Suzy and Dale Thomas. $25-45.*

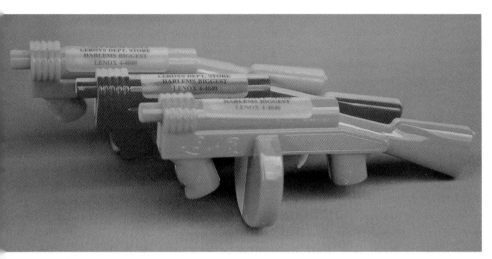

Lional Tomy Guns, 1950s. Made in U.S.A. Tags read a gift from Santa from Leroy's Department Store, Harlem, New York. Yellow, red, green, and blue plastic, 6.25" x 2.50". *Courtesy of Suzy and Dale Thomas. $25-35 each.*

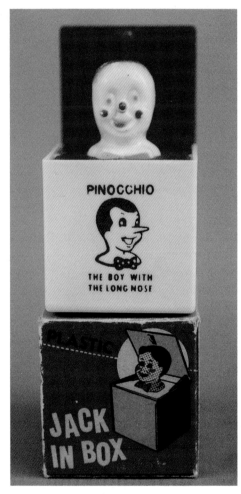

Pinocchio jack in box, party favor with original box, 1950s, Woodmere Toy Corporation. Red and cream color plastic with blue, red, and brown paint, 2.50" x 2.50". *Courtesy of Suzy and Dale Thomas. $45-55.*

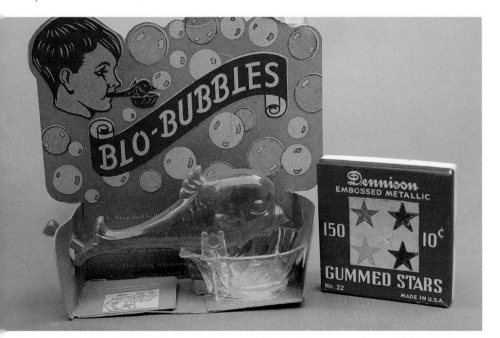

Knickerbocker Blo-bubbles Fish, party favor on original card, 1950s, embossed Knickerbocker Plastics Company, Glendale, California. Green and pink fluorescent plastic, card is 5" x 5". Dennison school stars. *Author's Collection. $30-45.*

A variety of hard plastic cows, late 1940s-1950s.

Puzzle key chain, party favor, Mexican on donkey, 1940s-1950s. Made in U.S.A. Orange, yellow, blue, green, red, and white plastic, original key chain, 2" x 2". *Author's Collection. $20-35.*

Christmas toys made by Plasticville U.S.A. for Lionel and other train sets, late 1940s. White, brown and black plastic, childhood toys of David Shock. *Author's Collection. $25 for all.*

Christmas toys, early plastic horses, 1940s. Made in U.S.A. Marbled plastic, painted over silver flash, 3" x 2.50". *Author's Collection. $15-20 each.*

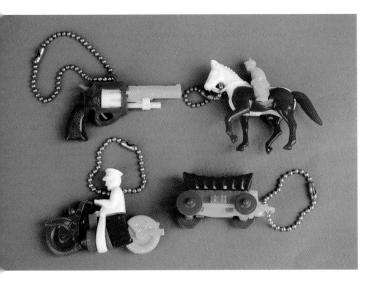

A variety of key chain puzzle, party favors, 1940s-1950s. Made in U.S.A. *Courtesy of Suzy and Dale. $20-35 each.*

Fire engine key chain puzzle, party favor, 1950s. Made in England on original card. Blue, red, green, and yellow plastic, card is 4" x 3". *Courtesy of Suzy and Dale Thomas. $20-40.*

Lional key chain puzzles, party favors, 1940s-1950s. Green, orange, red, white, and blue plastic, L. 2" x 1.50", R 3" x 1.50". *Courtesy of Suzy and Dale Thomas. $20-35.*

Small black plastic train, party favor, embossed. Made in U.S.A. Black plastic, came in all different colors, 12" x 2". *Author's Collection. $18-25.*

Irwin mechanical, Flutters the Butterfly novelty toy, 1950s. Red and black plastic body with wings of multi-colored vinyl, box is 4.50" x 6.75". *Courtesy of Bertram M. Cohen, Irwin Plastics Corporation Estate Collection. $35-55.*

Hard plastic Humpty Dumpty Christmas toy, 1953. Made in U.S.A. Yellow plastic with blue, red, and white paint, crown is missing. There are other parts inside of egg, box is 9" x 5". *Author's Collection. $65-85 complete.*

Above: Irwin flying bird in original box. Paper and plastic with launcher, box is 13.50" x 3". *Courtesy of Bertram M. Cohen, Irwin Plastics Corporation Estate Collection. $35-55.*

Right: Original box for the Irwin flying bird. *Courtesy of Bertram M. Cohen.*

Irwin mechanical crawling bear novelty toy, 1950s. Brown plastic with tan and black paint, wearing purple and red rompers, 5.50" x 4.75". *Courtesy of Bertram M. Cohen, Irwin Plastics Corporation Estate Collection. $85-100.*

Tommy Tune musical instrument, party favor, by Thomas Manufacturing Corporation, Newark, New Jersey, 1950s. Red plastic with paper tag, 5.50" x 5.50". *Courtesy of Suzy and Dale Thomas. $25-35.*

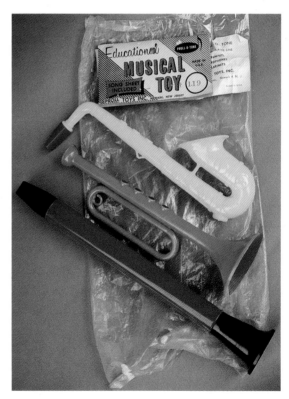

Mattel®, Hurdy Gurdy birthday present, 1954. Red and yellow plastic with a plastic monkey dressed in fur with a red and yellow yarn cord, box is 5.50" x 4.50". *Courtesy of Suzy and Dale Thomas. $65-85.*

Musical toy party favors, 1950s, Proll O Tone. Made in U.S.A. Yellow, black, and green plastic, sax and trumpet are 9" and clarinet is 12.50". *Courtesy of Suzy and Dale Thomas. $55-65, in original package.*

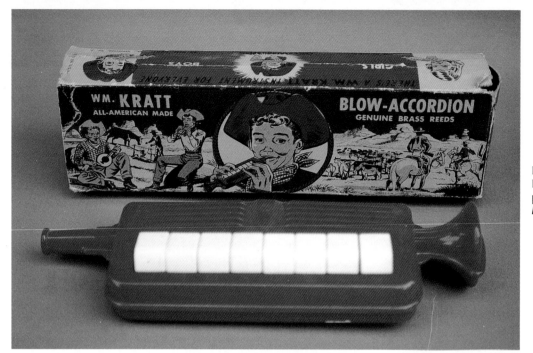

Blow Accordion birthday present, W. M. Kratt. Made in U.S.A. Red and white plastic, 9.25" x 3". *Courtesy of Suzy and Dale Thomas. $45-65 with original box.*

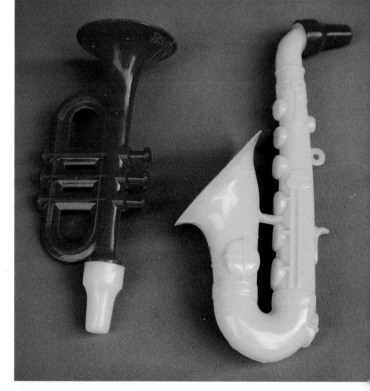

Above: Spec Toy French Horn, party favor, 1950s. Rust flash over white plastic, 6". *Courtesy of Suzy and Dale.* $25-35.

Right: Saxophone and trumpet party favors, 1950s, Trophy Company. Yellow and red plastic, sax 9", trumpet 8". *Courtesy of Suzy and Dale Thomas.* $35-45 each.

Spec Toy Trumpet, party favor, 1950s. Red, yellow, and green plastic with original tassel, 10". *Courtesy of Suzy and Dale Thomas.* $35-45.

Super circus band set, 1950s, Trophy Productions Company, Cleveland, Ohio. Seven instruments inside box, 14" x 13". *Courtesy of Suzy and Dale Thomas. $75-100 set.*

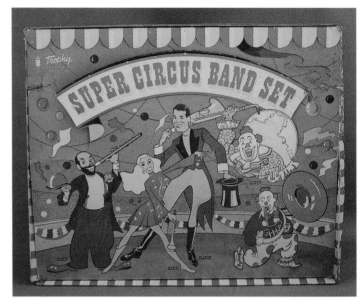

Super Circus Band set original box. *Courtesy of Suzy and Dale Thomas.*

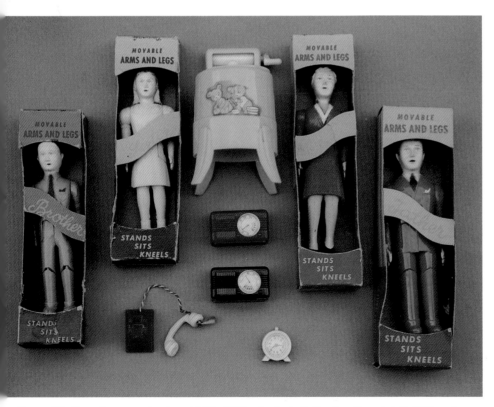

Renwal Dolls and accessories, late 1940s-1950s. *Author's Collection. Boxed dolls $50 each. Washing machine $45. Small accessories $10-25 each.*

Pig cookie cutter party favor, not embossed. Made in U.S.A. Red plastic with black paint (one of a set) 3" x 1.5" *Author's Collection. $3-5 each.*

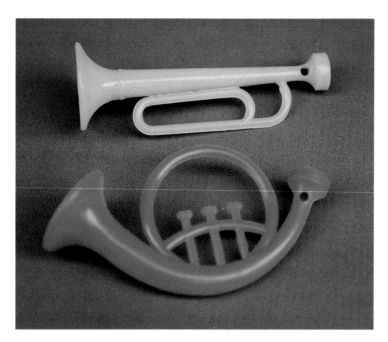

Small E. Rosen candy container whistles, 1950s. Yellow and green plastic, 3.50". *Courtesy of Suzy and Dale Thomas. $18-25 each.*

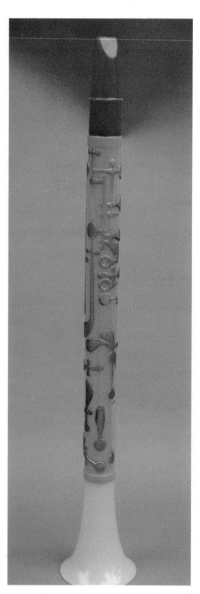

Spec Toy clarinet, party favor, 1950s. Yellow, red and green plastic, 15" long. *Courtesy of Suzy and Dale Thomas. $35-50.*

Red Riding Hood rattle, 1950s, not embossed. Made in U.S.A. Red plastic with yellow, black, and flesh paint, 4" x 2". *Author's Collection. $15-20.*

Small E. Rosen candy container whistle, 1950s. Red plastic, 3.50". *Author's Collection. $18-25.*

Bear rattle, 1950s, not embossed. Made in U.S.A. Red plastic, 4" x 2". Courtesy of Suzy and Dale Thomas. $15-20.

Best *Plastics* baby room bear lamp, embossed, *Best* U.S.A. Blue plastic with red paint and googly eyes, 8" x 4". *Author's Collection.* $45-65.

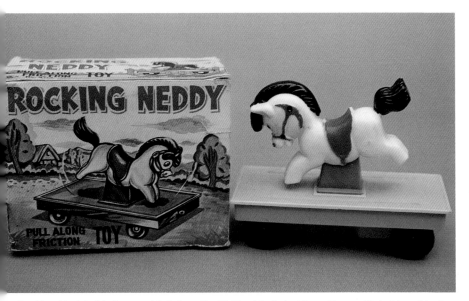

Rocking Neddy friction toy birthday gift, 1960s. Made in Hong Kong. Pink, blue, black, and white plastic with red and black paint, 5" x 4.50". *Author's Collection.* $20-35.

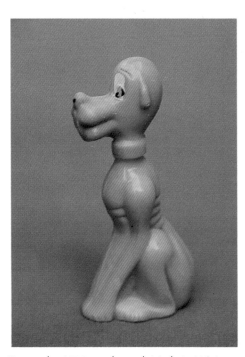

Dog rattle, 1950s, embossed. Made in U.S.A. Blue plastic with white and black paint, 5" x 2.50". *Author's Collection.* $15-20.

Baby cup with decal of cat, 1950s, not embossed. Made in U.S.A. Pink plastic, 5" x 4". *Author's Collection.* $15-20.

Underwriters' Laboratories Inc., baby room elephant lamp, 1940s-1950s. White and pink plastic, 6" x 7". *Author's Collection.* $50-65.

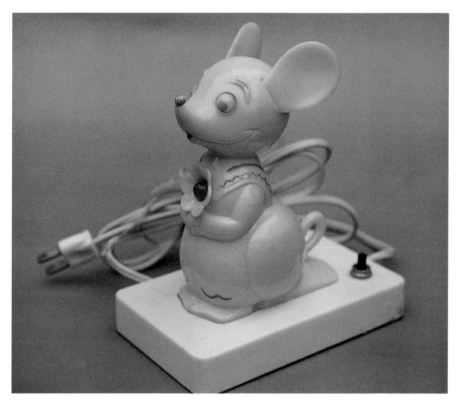

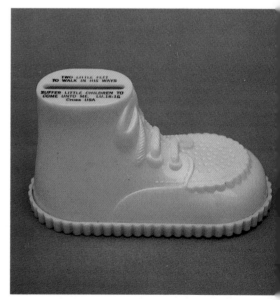

Baby shoe bank, 1950s, not embossed. Made in U.S.A. Pink and blue plastic, 5" x 3". *Author's Collection.* $15-20.

Underwriters' Laboratories Inc., baby room mouse lamp, 1940s-1950s. White and pink plastic with blue paint, 6" x 6". *Author's Collection.* $50-65.

Baby bank, not embossed,1950s-1960s. Made in U.S.A. Pink plastic, the baby on the top is vinyl, 9" x 7". *Author's Collection. $20-35.*

Baby bank,1950s, not embossed. Made in U.S.A. Blue and flesh plastic with red, white, and blue paint, 9" x 5". *Author's Collection. $25-40.*

Irwin Baby Beauregard rattle, 1950s. Flesh plastic with white, black, and brown, the milk goes up and down as he drinks, 5" x 2". *Courtesy of Bertram M. Cohen, Irwin Plastics Corporation Estate Collection. $40-55.*

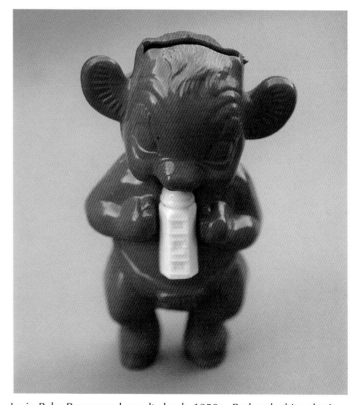

Irwin Baby Beauregard novelty bank, 1950s. Red and white plastic, 5" x 2". *Author's Collection. $40-55.*

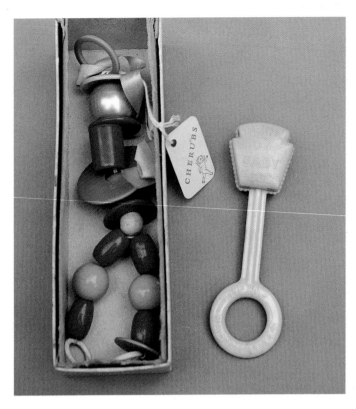

Baby toys, the one on the right is Heinz Food Corporation and the one on the left is tagged Cherubs, 1940s-1950s. L 7" x 2", R 5" x 1.50". *Author's Collection. L. $20-35, R. $15-20.*

Knickerbocker baby shower stork, party decoration. White plastic with orange, blue, green, black and flesh paint, 6.50" x 5". *Courtesy of Suzy and Dale Thomas. $20-35 with baby.*

Above: A variety of 1940s-1950s hard plastic Plakie and "Made in U.S.A." baby toys.

Left: Bakelite baby toy, 1930s. Made in U.S.A. Red, yellow, green, black, and orange plastic with pink, black, and red paint, original Wunsch family Christmas tree decoration. *Author's Collection. $125.*

Cry baby novelty toy, late 1940s-1950s baby shower gift. You pull the lollypop pop out of his mouth, his head rises and his face changes to a crying face. *Author's Collection. $45-60.*

Irwin Cat and Kewpie celluloid baby rattles, 1930s-1940s. *Courtesy of Bertram M. Cohen, Irwin Plastics Corporation Estate Collection. L. $45-55, R. $45-65.*

Irwin baby carriage sample tag. *Courtesy of Bertram M. Cohen.*

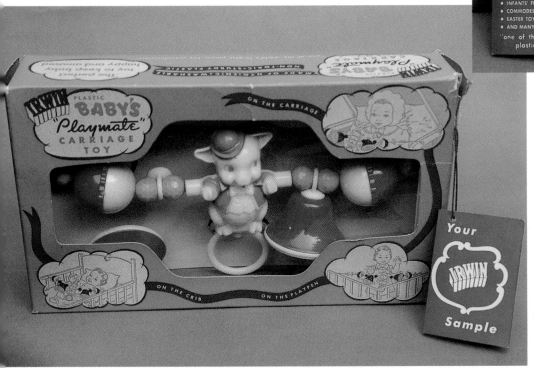

Irwin baby carriage toy, 1950s. Yellow, blue, red and white plastic with blue paint, box is 11" x 6.50". *Courtesy of Bertram M. Cohen, Irwin Plastics Corporation Estate Collection, $45-65.*

149

Building blocks, 1940s-1950s, Banner U.S.A. Green, yellow, blue, pink, red and clear plastic.
Author's Collection. $3-5.

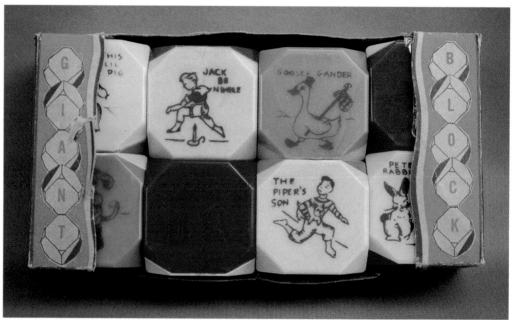

Plastic nursery rhyme blocks, 1950s, Plastic Toy and Novelty Corporation. Green, red, pink, and yellow plastic with blue pictures, box is 9.50" x 5". *Courtesy of Suzy and Dale Thomas. $35-50.*

Box for nursery rhyme blocks, Plastic Toy and Novelty Corporation.

Christmas telephone, 1950s. Made in U.S.A. Red and green plastic with original yarn cord, 7" x 5". *Courtesy of Suzy and Dale Thomas.* *$25-35.*

Easter telephone, 1950s. Made in U.S.A. Blue and pink plastic with original yarn cord, 7" x 5". *Courtesy of Suzy and Dale Thomas. $25-35.*

Above: Bosco novelty clown bottle, 1960s. Red and white vinyl with black paint, 5" x 3" in diameter. *Author's Collection. $15-25.*

Below: Metal bottom of Bosco bottle.

E. Rosen clown lamp, 1950s, embossed Rosbro Plastics. White, red, and blue plastic with blue, red, and black paint, 7" x 3". *Courtesy of Suzy and Dale Thomas. $95-125.*

A trio of E. Rosen yellow clown candy containers, 1950s, embossed Rosbro Plastics. *Author's Collection. Off wheels, $65-85; on wheels, $85-115.*

E. Rosen clown candy container on wheels, 1950s, embossed Rosbro Plastics. Red, green, and yellow plastic with black paint, 6" x 3". *Courtesy of Suzy and Dale Thomas. $85-115.* 55

E. Rosen clown candy container on wheels, 1950s, embossed Rosbro Plastics. White, red, green, and yellow plastic with red, yellow, and black paint, 6" x 3". *Author's Collection. $85-115.*

A trio of E. Rosen clown candy containers, 1950s, embossed Rosbro Plastics. Off wheels Halloween Zook, 5" x 3", $65-85, policeman on wheels, 6" x 3", $95-130, pink clown on wheels, 6" x 3", $85-115. *Courtesy of Richard Miller, Photo by Richard Miller.*

Irwin celluloid clown rattles, 1930s-1940s. *Courtesy of Bertram M. Cohen, Irwin Plastics Corporation Estate Collection. L. $85-115, R. $95-125.*

Tico Toys clown novelty bank on blue wheels, late 1940s, not embossed. Yellow plastic with red and white paint, original novelty clown bank tag, 7.50" x 6.75". *Author's Collection. $375-450.*

Clown baby rattle, 1950s, not embossed. Made in U.S.A. Pink plastic, 4.50" x 2". *Author's Collection. $20-30.*

Tico Toys clown novelty Halloween bank on yellow wheels, late 1940s, not embossed. Orange plastic with black and green paint, 7.50" x 6.75". *Courtesy of Mark and Judy Craven. $375-450.*

153

Irwin licensed Walt Disney Donald Duck® hard plastic Noddy Toy, 1950s, 5.50". *Courtesy of Bertram M. Cohen, Irwin Plastics Corporation Estate Collection. $200-250 in box.*

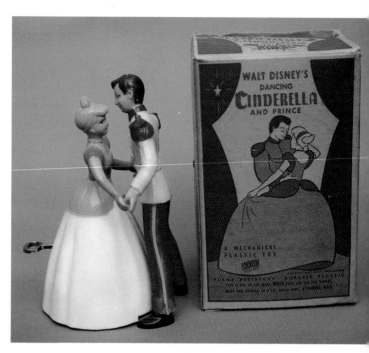

Irwin licensed dancing Disney® Cinderella and Prince, 1950s, hard plastic. Painted white, red, cream, flesh, yellow, and black paint, box is 7" x 5". *Courtesy of Bertram M. Cohen, Irwin Plastics Corporation Estate Collection. $175 200 in box.*

Clown puppet, 1950s. Made in U.S.A. Yellow plastic with blue and red paint, original clown outfit, 6.50". *Author's Collection. $35-50.*

Irwin mechanical wind up policeman blowing whistle, hard plastic, 1950s, 6.50". *Courtesy of Bertram M. Cohen, Irwin Plastics Corporation Estate Collection. $125-150.*

Hard plastic coasters and plastic party ware, late 1940s-1950s. Made in U.S.A. *Author's Collection. Coasters $15-25, table ware $5-8.*

Irwin 1940s Popeye® nonflammable celluloid wobble toy, 7.50". *Courtesy of Bertram M. Cohen, Irwin Plastics Corporation Estate Collection. $155-185.*

Painted pink flamingo and palm tree juice glasses, 1950s. Turquoise and pink plastic with red, pink, green, blue, brown, yellow, and black paint, 2.50" x 2.50". *Author's Collection. $15-20.*

Irwin licensed Mickey Mouse® Noddy Toy, 1950s, hard plastic, 7.50". *Courtesy of Bertram M. Cohen, Irwin Plastics Corporation Estate Collection. $150-175 without box.*

155

Chef novelty light switch plates, 1950s, made in the Leominster, Massachusetts area. *Author's Collection. $10 each.*

Novelty light switch poodle dog, 1950s, made in the Leominster, Massachusetts area. *Author's Collection. $10.*

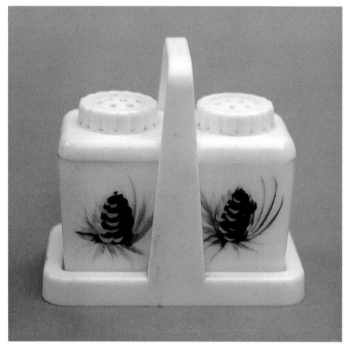

Picnic salt and pepper shakes with pine cone decals, 1950s. Made in U.S.A. Yellow and white plastic, 3.50" x 3.50". *Author's Collection. $15-25.*

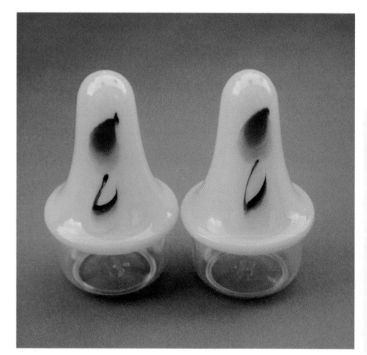

Hand painted (at the factory) salt and pepper shakers, party ware. Made in U.S.A. *Author's Collection. $15-18.*

Kitchen ware cookie jar with flowered decals, 1950s. Made in U.S.A. *Author's Collection.* $25-40.

Halloween cat candy container and kitchen cat wall pocket, 1950s, not embossed, made in the Pawtucket, Providence, Rhode Island area. Cat is black plastic with orange and white paint, 3.50" x 3", wall pocket is red and white plastic with black paint, 5" x 4.50". *Author's Collection. Halloween cat is $40-50, wall pocket is $18-20.*

Salt and pepper shakers, 1950s. Made in U.S.A. 1960s handpainted party/picnic dishes made in Hong Kong. *Author's Collection. Glass shakers $3-5; pear shakers $15-20; dishes $15-25 each.*

Souvenir cat salt and pepper shakers from the Abraham Lincoln home in Springfield, Illinois, with matching hand painted wall pocket dish, 1950s. *Author's Collection. Cats $25-35, dish $20-35.*

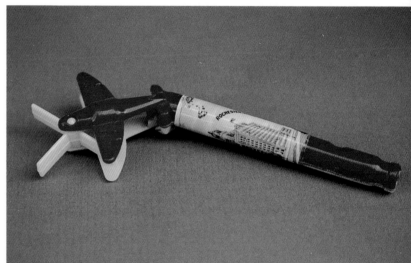

Picnic salt and pepper shakers, 1950s, hard plastic, Commonwealth Plastics. *Author's Collection. $10-15.*

Souvenir salt and pepper shakers, 1950s . Made in U.S.A. *Author's Collection. $10-15.*

Souvenir airplane whistle from Rochester, Minnesota. Red and yellow plastic, the airplane moves as you blow the whistle, 6" x 2.5". *Courtesy of Suzy and Dale Thomas. $25-35.*

Souvenir dresser bank, 1940s-1950s. Made in U.S.A., came from South Bend, Indiana. Brown marbled plastic, 6" x 4.50". *Author's Collection. $25-35.*

Hard plastic picnic sand toys, 1950s . Made in U.S.A. Red, green, blue, and yellow plastic, 4.75" x 3". *Courtesy of Suzy and Dale Thomas. $25-35 set.*

Picnic party ware, 1940s-1950s, . Made in U.S.A. Yellow, green, blue, and red plastic in original box, box is 16" x 16". *Author's Collection. $25-40.*

Picnic and party ware, 1940s-1950s. Made in U.S.A. Green, yellow and red plastic with green and red paint, these are older salt and peppers and they come apart in the middle instead of having plugs. *Author's Collection. Pear salts $20-35, apple salts $15-25, napkin holder $15-20.*

Picnic and party ware, 1940s-1950s. Made in U.S.A. Red, green, and yellow plastic, there are no salt and pepper plugs, the older novelties came apart in the middle to put condiments or salt and pepper inside. The newer plastic novelties like these have vinyl salt and pepper plugs. *Author's Collection. Green pepper $15-25, tomato salts $15-25, corn salts $5-10, rocket salts $15-22.*

BIBLIOGRAPHY

Anderton, Johana Gast, *Twentieth Century Dolls*, Kansas City,
    Missouri, Trojan Press Inc., 1971.
Apkarian-Russel, Pamela E., *More Halloween Collectibles*,
    Atglen, Pa., Schiffer Publishing Ltd., 1995.
Garrison, Susan Ann, *Raggedy Ann and Andy Family Album*,
    Westchester, Pa., Schiffer Publishing, 1989.
Hake, Ted, *Hakes' Guide to TV Collectibles*, Radnor, Pa.,
    Wallace Homestead Book Co., 1990.
Judd, Polly and Pam, *Hard Plastic Dolls, Book I*, Cumberland,
    Maryland, Hobby House Press, 1985.
Judd, Polly and Pam, *Hard Plastic Dolls, Book II*, Grantsville,
    Maryland, Hobby House Press, 1989.
Schiffer, Margaret, *Holidays, Toys and Decorations*, Atglen, Pa.,
    Schiffer Publishing Ltd., 1985.
Schneider, Stuart, *Halloween In America*, Atglen, Pa., Schiffer
    Publishing Ltd., 1995.
Pinkerton, Charlene, *Halloween Favorites In Plastic*, Atglen,
    Pa., Schiffer Publishing Ltd., 1998.

RESOURCES

American Plastics History Association, Granville, Ohio.
Glendale, Califonia Public Library.
Plastics Museum, Leominster, Mass.
Providence Rhode Island Public Library.

Author's Collection.